North American
INDIAN CHIEFS

North American
INDIAN CHIEFS

General Editor: Karl Nagelfell

JG PRESS

Published in the USA 1995 by JG Press
Distributed by World Publications, Inc.

The JG Press imprint is a trademark of JG Press, Inc.
455 Somerset Avenue
North Dighton, MA 02764

Produced by
Brompton Books Corporation
15 Sherwood Place
Greenwich, Connecticut 06830

ISBN 1-57215-055-6

Printed in China

Designed by Bill Yenne

All photographs are supplied through the courtesy of the Library of
Congress with the following exceptions:
The Bettmann Archive 11, 13, 29, 31, 32, 37
Brompton Picture Library 10, 12, 14, 15, 16, 17, 18, 22, 24, 25, 26-27, 28,
    30, 40-41, 42
Lincoln Library and Museum, Louis A Warren Collection 34
Museum of New Mexico 6, 63
National Archives 58, 59, 61, 62 (bottom)
National Gallery of Art 1
Smithsonian Institution 7, 8, 9, 21, 23, 28, 30, 33, 35, 36, 39, 43, 44, 45,
    46, 47, 48, 49 (both), 52 (top), 53, 54, 56, 57, 60-61
Smithsonian Institution, National Collection of Fine Arts 4-5
Smithsonian Institution, National Museum of the American Indian 51,
    54-55, 62 (top)

PAGE ONE: WHITE CLOUD, CHIEF OF THE IOWA, AS PAINTED BY GEORGE CATLIN
DURING ONE OF HIS SURVEYS OF THE PLAINS IN THE 1830S.

PAGE TWO: CHIEF JOSEPH OF THE NEZ PERCE, PHOTOGRAPHED BY EDWARD
CURTIS.

THESE PAGES: GEORGE CATLIN'S PAINTING OF A COMANCHE WARRIOR IN COM-
BAT WITH AN OSAGE ENEMY.

TABLE OF CONTENTS

PREFACE

By Tintinmeetsa (Willouskin), Chief of the Umatillas
in comments made in 1909 at a commemoration of
the Battle of the Little Bighorn

This country all looks familiar to me because, in my younger days, I travelled over these prairies fighting the Sioux Indians who had stolen horses from my people. Again I have travelled all over this country many times, long years ago, as we came here to hunt the buffalo.

I had a number of fast horses, with which I could easily kill as many buffalo as I wanted, but I killed only as many as I needed to last for a few days. When I came here the other day to meet all these chiefs, and I looked at this country for the last time, I felt lonesome when I saw how it was all changed, and all of the buffalo gone out of the country, for I could still see traces of these large animals.

It is easy for an old hunter to discover these buffalo trails, for they all walked in the same place, and now the rains of many moons have cut those trails deep, just as if a man had been irrigating some field. I can scarcely see, but my eyes could find the old trail. The buffalo has gone, and I am going soon.

BELOW: AN ARAPAHO CAMP ON THE CANADIAN RIVER IN WHAT IS NOW OKLAHOMA. *OPPOSITE:* 'WAR MEMORIES', A PHOTOGRAPH TAKEN BY JOSEPH KOSSUTH DIXON BETWEEN 1908 AND 1917.

INTRODUCTION

As we gain a greater awareness of the importance of Native American culture, and of the importance of the role of Native Americans in American history, their leaders emerge at last as the monumental figures they really were.

Hiawatha forged the Iroquois Confederacy, an alliance more successful than its European counterparts of the era. Joseph Brant (Thayendanegea) of the Mohawks was educated in London, and designed an eighteenth century framework of an alliance with Britain. Tecumseh of the Shawnee also played an important role in unifying the Native people of the Southeast a generation later.

Osceola of the Seminoles and Red Cloud of the Dakota Sioux are remembered today as being among the great statesmen of the nineteenth century. Crazy Horse was a revered spiritual leader. Sitting Bull of the Dakota and Geronimo of the Apache are recognized as among America's great military leaders. Joseph of the Nez Perce was one of North American history's most eloquent orators.

The legacy of the great chiefs is today more than just a relic of the past. Indeed, their words and their deeds are a living reality of our collective past, and an enduring reminder that America's Native peoples were once free and independent nations, and their leaders were truly important and diplomatically skilled heads of state.

Today, a new generation of Native leaders are facing new challenges, finding pride in a great heritage, and reclaiming the majesty of their forefathers, who were among North America's greatest leaders.

BELOW: A DETAIL FROM GEORGE CATLIN'S PORTRAIT OF BLACK MOCCASIN, CHIEF OF THE HIDATSA. *OPPOSITE:* A PORTRAIT OF HORSE CHIEF OF THE PAWNEE, PAINTED BY CATLIN IN 1832.

HIAWATHA

The area that is now the northeastern United States is the traditional home of the Native American peoples of the Iroquoian linguistic group. These are principally the six peoples of New York State, the Seneca, Oneida, Onondaga, Cayuga, Mohawk and Tuscarora, but also including their neighbors, the Huron, Erie and Susquehanna.

Settled in the Mohawk Valley of New York, the Iroquois people began to increase and to prosper. They fortified their villages with stockades, which some of the first European visitors called castles. According to legend, the first French visitors to the Iroquois were served popcorn over which hot maple syrup was poured. One of the party wrote letters to friends in France, praising this new 'snow food' and advocating its introduction into the home country.

Conditions were such that by the middle sixteenth century, a great political leader came upon the scene to unite the Iroquois. He is known to history as Hiawatha. He probably was born about 1500, and was active until about 1570. According to tradition, he went through the Mohawk Valley, advocating a new order of brotherly feeling between the peoples, not necessarily peace for all men, but rather a union of relatives.

ABOVE: THIS CLASSIC SCENE WAS TAKEN FROM LONGFELLOW'S FAMOUS POEM, 'HIAWATHA.' *OPPOSITE:* A FANCIFUL VIEW OF AN IROQUOIS HUNTING PARTY.

The traditions of Native American life had always been for absolute freedom of action, and each community was jealous of this right. Every small group functioned for itself, so each Iroquois people hesitated to bind itself to a majority vote. The idea of a confederacy did not appeal to them.

Apparently, Hiawatha was so persistent that five peoples — Mohawk, Seneca, Cayuga, Onondaga and Oneida — finally agreed to his proposed federation.

The scheme Hiawatha devised was admirable. It was an unwritten constitution authorizing the election of a representative body and formulating rules for calling it into session. The vote was by people. If war was to be declared, the vote must be unanimous. Disputes between peoples were to be arbitrated and not settled by violence. This unwritten constitution, admired by colonial statesmen, gave each people almost complete independence but at the same time bound it to respect the wishes of others.

Europeans eventually spoke of these peoples as the Five Nations — or the 'Five Civilized Tribes' — recognizing that they were independent, but nevertheless were in a league for defense and offense. In about 1715, the Tuscarora entered into the confederacy upon the same terms, thus changing the designation to the Six Nations.

After Hiawatha's death, as the power of the Five Nations grew, his fame grew with it, until he was believed a super-natural rather than a natural man. European people were disposed to look upon him as little short of an Native American deity and, in turn, the esteemed nineteenth century American poet Henry Wadsworth Longfellow chose his name for the chief character of his beautiful poem, intended by him as a work of fiction, a kind of historical novel in verse.

While the famous League of the Iroquois was a peaceful union for the Six Nations, it was also a military alliance against neighboring peoples.

Nevertheless, students of politics and government have found much to admire in the working of the League, and there is some historical evidence that knowledge of the League influenced the colonies in their first efforts to form a confederacy and later to write a constitution.

In 1744 Connecticut and Pennsylvania negotiated with certain Native Americans to adjust land claims, during which proceedings an Oneida chief suggested to the colonial delegates that since the League had worked so well with the Iroquois, something similar be set up to govern the relations of the colonies. There is some evidence to indicate that at another conference in Albany, in 1775, an Iroquois speaker made a similar suggestion.

POWHATAN

The story of America's native leaders is, unfortunately, dependent on the interpretation of outsiders — the white Europeans that recorded what has come to us as the recorded history of North America. The stories of the leaders that predated the arrival of the Europeans is lost in the smoky haze of legend, and historic fact begins with those great chiefs with whom the Europeans first had contact.

The first permanent settlement in North America was the English colony at Jamestown, which was established here on the Virginia coast in 1607. The land was, of course, already occupied. The people who lived here were known as the Powhatan. Their 'king,' as he was described by the English, was known as Wahunsenacah, or Wahusonacook.

Because Native Americans frequently kept their true name a secret and went by an alias or nickname in order to prevent enemies from seizing the essence of their spirit, Wahunsenacah was called Chief Powhatan. By the time of Jamestown's founding, King Powhatan, a powerful man in his mid-50s, ruled a 'Powhatan Confederation' that included 32 peoples, 200 villages and perhaps 10,000 people of seaboard Virginia. Powhatan's own village was a day's ride from Jamestown, at the falls of the James River, near what is now Richmond.

The English colonial leader Captain John Smith described Powhatan as well-proportioned and able-bodied, indeed strong. There was a real mix of nobility and serenity about him. The 19th century historian, Wyndham Peterson, described him correctly as a leader who was stern yet affectionate at times, and brave, though also wary and subtle.

Smith was determined to maintain good relations with the Native Americans. In this, he was backed up by the Virginia Company. Its London directors thought, correctly, that peace in Virginia would be cheaper than war. Smith stood his ground when Powhatan withheld corn, and he was infinitely resourceful in the face of the hunger of his people.

To attempt to seal their friendship, Smith actually crowned Powhatan king in 1609. As strange as this exercise must appear in hindsight, Smith complained that the chief was more interested in his gifts than in the copper crown, with all its significant symbolism, which Smith placed on his graying head.

Meanwhile, Powhatan taught the English to cultivate corn and tobacco, but sometimes refused them corn in starving times in order to keep them dependent upon him.

However, after samples of tobacco sent to London as early as 1613 turned into a major export trade, the colonists became more powerful. Powhatan came to know Captain John Smith to be a formidable adversary.

Soon after he arrived, Smith fell into Powhatan's hands while exploring and mapping the colony. The Englishman was a former professional soldier who had fought in campaigns throughout Europe, including those against the Turks in Transylvania. He had been captured and enslaved by them, so hardships were scarcely anything new to him.

As legend has it, Smith was about to be put to death by having his head bashed, when Powhatan's 12-year-old daughter, Pocahontas, intervened to save his life. The incident is possibly apocryphal and has been dismissed as 'an exploded story' by many, but it may very well have happened.

It has also been said that Powhatan's daughter inherited all of her father's best traits without his harsh qualities. Certainly her name is one of the most familiar of Native American folklore.

Her real name was, however, Matoaka, but she did not want it used by strangers. Smith wrote: 'The Native Americans did think that, did we know her real name, we should have the power of casting an evil eye upon her.' Thus it was that she was called by an intriguing nickname, Pocahontas, meaning 'playful.'

The chief's daughter was interested in the English and their culture. As a child, Pocahontas had liked to play with colonists' children, turning cartwheels in the dusty streets of Jamestown. As she grew older, she not only donned buckskins but matured into a remarkably adept 'ambassadress' for her father. Since she frequented Jamestown as much as her own village, she was able to successfully restore captives to one side or another.

At one point, she brought provisions to the hungry residents of Jamestown, and was virtually adopted by the grateful and hard-pressed settlers.

Smith wrote of her: 'She, under God, was the instrument to preserve this colony from death, famine, and utter confusion. Blessed Pocahontas, the great King's daughter of Virginia, oft saved my life.'

Later warning Smith of an impending raid, subsequently cancelled by her father, she probably saved Jamestown for a second time. Unfortunately, when Smith was injured in an accident and went to England in 1609, relations deteriorated immediately.

According to William Strachey, a historian of the Commonwealth, the Native Americans, possibly stimulated by the Spanish from Florida, rose in war and 'did spoil and murder all they encountered.' He wrote of a queen of the Powhatan Confederacy who is said to have killed 14 men in the winter of 1610.

Retaliation was automatic and swift. The English burned her village and killed her and some of her warriors in a pursuit through the woods. In an attack on 30 colonists, only Henry Spelman was spared because Pocahontas, in a re-enactment of the Captain Smith episode, intervened to save his life. He lived for years among the Potomac Indians and was later a skillful interpreter for the colonists. Pocahontas withdrew and did not willingly visit Jamestown after Smith left.

In 1614, however, the peace that had existed between the Powhatan Confederacy and Jamestown was guaranteed when Chief Powhatan permitted his daughter to marry First Secretary John Rolfe. Pocahontas now took the Christian name Rebecca and moved with her husband to England. She died there in 1617, having given birth to a son, Thomas Rolfe.

When Wahunsenacah himself died, a year after his daughter in 1618, the mantle of 'king' of the Powhatan passed to his brother, Chief Opechancanough, who had little fondness for Jamestown. He attacked in 1622 and thus began a cycle of violence and distrust that came to a head in April 1644, when some 400-500 English colonists were killed, mostly on the York and Pamunkey rivers, where the old chief was in personal command. But while he had been mustering his strength over two decades, the Virginia population had climbed to 8000. The immediate defeat stung the colony, but was far from crushing. In fact, the English, under Governor Sir William Berkeley, quickly seized the initiative from the Native Americans and drove them back into the forest.

Chief Opechancanough was defeated, captured and borne to Jamestown. He lay on his litter, still as the death which he

ABOVE: A CONTEMPORARY PORTRAIT OF POCAHONTAS, ALSO KNOWN AS REBECCA ROLFE, AND HER SON THOMAS. *OPPOSITE:* A PORTRAIT OF POWHATAN IN HIS CEREMONIAL GARB.

anticipated. His eyes were closed and some said that the ancient one no longer had the strength to open his eyelids. Suddenly, a guard, probably a militiaman who had lost a relative, turned his weapon and fired, point blank. The ball did not kill Opechancanough, and he pulled himself to his feet and ordered his startled guards to send for Berkeley.

When the Governor arrived, it was to receive a scolding: 'If it had been my fortune to take Sir William Berkeley prisoner, I would not have meanly exposed him as a show to my people.'

According to legend, the Chief lay quietly down and died. All Native American hope of extinguishing Jamestown died with Opechancanough. But guerrilla warfare continued. The General Assembly passed an act for 'perpetual warre,' but this was replaced with a peace treaty in 1646 with the new chief, Necotowance.

MASSASOIT and METACOMET

In the folklore of those Americans of English descent, no event is more firmly associated with their ancestors' arrival in North America than the landing of the Pilgrims at Plymouth in 1620.

Seen through the eyes of Native Americans, this event is the incursion of strangers upon the lands of the Wampanoag people, whose 'king' (as the English liked to describe his 'office') was the great Chief Ousamequin. The Pilgrims found that he was the ruler of much of what we now know as New England. Though his real name was Ousamequin (Yellow Feather), he was addressed by his title, Massasoit (Great Chief). One settler described him in 1621 as being 'a very lusty man, in his best years, an able body, grave of countenance, and spare in speech.'

Massasoit's home and seat of power was at Pokanoket, near present Mount Hope, Rhode Island, but he had contact with Plymouth colony leader Captain Myles Standish as early as 1620. Massasoit may have also met Captain John Smith while the latter was exploring and mapping the New England coast.

Massasoit was a reasonable man. He permitted sea captains to collect English castaways he had held prisoner, and sensed that peace and accommodation were preferable to war in dealing with the strangers. He became their friend and ally. On 22 March 1621 Massasoit brought his brother, Quadequina, and two leading chiefs, Samoset and Squanto, to a meeting in Plymouth.

Samoset startled some settlers by walking out of the woods and greeting them with 'Welcome, Englishmen.' He had picked up a few words in their tongue from fishermen on the coast.

Samoset lived until 1653 and Massasoit until 1661, but Squanto, who is said to have helped Plymouth celebrate the 'first Thanksgiving,' died in 1622.

The harmonious relations between European and Native that is commemorated in the Thanksgiving celebration soon deteriorated into a series of bloody conflicts that pitted the English settlers in the Northeast against the Narragansett, Nipmuk, Pequot and Wampanoag peoples. The first of these conflicts, the Pequot War of 1636, set the stage for what was to be known as King Philip's War.

King Philip, whose real name was Metacomet, was born in 1639, the youngest son of the venerable Massasoit. Having succeeded his father, Metacomet tried to accommodate the English settlers, who had gradually begun to outnumber the Native Americans. In 1671, the English accused him of plotting against them and forced his people to give up their weapons.

King Philip's War ensued, and Metacomet found himself opposite Benjamin Church, a Rhode Islander who'd always been a good friend of the Native Americans. He really knew them, especially the 'queen' or squaw-sachem, Awashonks, of the Sakonnets. It was the queen who warned him of Metacomet 'conspiracy,' and it was he who cautioned her not

ABOVE: MASSASOIT AND JOHN CARVER CONCLUDING THEIR TREATY OF FRIENDSHIP. *OPPOSITE:* A HEROIC PORTRAIT OF METACOMET HOLDING AN ENGLISH FLINTLOCK RIFLE. *OPPOSITE BOTTOM:* THE DEATH OF METACOMET IN 1676.

to ally her people with Metacomet. (For a time, she went along with Church, but later, disastrously, joined Metacomet.)

Church urged full use of Native American allies as scouts, trackers, interpreters and soldier-warriors, especially since the Colonials were clumsy fighters in marshes or woods. They preferred open country, describing swamp combat as 'fighting wild beasts in their dens.'

Church urged that troops be sent to join him at Pocasset Neck, but he found the Native Americans he was after, all too many of them. Luckily for him and his men, Metacomet's marksmen were terrible shots.

In July 1675, Metacomet was trapped in the cedars of Pocasset Swamp near the Taunton River, but he simply sent out some decoys to lure the colonists deeper into the swamp, and then ambushed them into a hasty retreat. When the colonists decided to starve King Metacomet into submission, the Native Americans collected canoes and slipped away to the Connecticut River. Metacomet counterattacked and forced the colonists into Brookfield, and burned every other structure. A sudden downpour put out the fire.

Among the stranger legends to come out of King Philip's War was that of the siege of Hadley, Massachusetts. The citizens, locked in the meeting house against Wampanoags, were led in a counterattack by a mysterious stranger. According to the legend, the man who seemed to appear out of nowhere was none other than the killer of Charles I, William Goffe, who had fled to Connecticut after the Restoration.

Meanwhile, New York's then-governor, Sir Edmund Andros, persuaded the Mohawks not to join Metacomet, but the Narragansetts, with 3000 to 5000 men under Chief Canonchet, threw in their lot with Metacomet. This proved a disaster, for during the Great Swamp Battle of December

1675, the Narragansetts were smashed and largely obliterated as a people.

Metacomet continued the fight, so confident of success that he ordered his people to plant their corn in the abandoned fields of the colonists. However, even as Benjamin Church was still recovering from the wounds he had received in battle, Metacomet's Sakonnet allies turned on him and offered to join Church. He made a successful attack on Metacomet's head-quarters in July 1676. Church almost captured Metacomet, and left him with only a few loyal followers. This led to the end of King Philip's War.

On 11 August 1676, a disgruntled Native American offered to guide Church to Metacomet's hiding place. The next day, Church's men surrounded the swamp in which he was camped. The chief heard them coming and ran for a secret trail. One of Church's men, Caleb Cook, aimed at Metacomet but his gun misfired. Alderman, the Native American who'd betrayed Metacomet, then fired a double charge into the chief's chest. He fell, face down, in a pool of muddy water.

PONTIAC

It was in 1755 that Pontiac, the 35-year-old chief of the Ottawa, came to the forefront as a major political leader in the Great Lakes country, the area of the 'old Northwest.' He did so by forging an alliance between his own people and the Chippewa, Potawatomi and his mother's people, the Miami. He also maintained good relations with the French, who were at that time engaged in a struggle with the English for influence in the region.

By 1700, the French had developed a policy not to attempt to colonize the country between Louisiana and Detroit, but tried to induce the Native Americans to live in peace with each other. The French were at home in the network of lakes and streams which made it easy to pass and thus keep communications open from Quebec to New Orleans. Their policy was moderately successful, because in suggesting resistance to the advance of the English frontier they provided the catalyst for the French and Indian War of 1754-1763.

Pontiac was a hereditary chief of the Ottawa, but it was not through heredity or custom that he led many diverse peoples into a long combat, sustained with great courage. It was by right of his powers of leadership.

The fall of Quebec to the English gave a new impetus to the advance of the English frontier. Settlers swarmed the Appalachians, alarming the people within Pontiac's alliance.

Pontiac had been a consistent friend of the French, and he led the Ottawa and Chippewa warriors at Fort Duquesne at the time of British General Edward Braddock's defeat there in 1755. Apparently, the first documentation of him is when Major Robert Rodgers' Rangers conveyed news of the capitulation of Quebec. Pontiac met with them and told them 'I shall stand in your way till morning.'

When it became clear that the English would not treat him as an ally, Pontiac forged an alliance of peoples with the French. The spring of 1763 was set for the beginning of warfare. Major Gladwyn, in command of the little garrison at Detroit, heard the rumors, but refused to credit them.

Tradition has it that a Native American girl called Catherine, who had won his favor, revealed to him the plan which Pontiac and his braves had decided upon. Coming to the fort with a pair of moccasins which she had beaded for him, Catherine told the commandant to expect a visit from the warriors in apparently friendly guise. Admitted to the fort, they would await a given signal to bring out their concealed weapons for use upon the unsuspecting soldiers.

The story proved to be true, and on 7 May, Pontiac and his warriors presented themselves before the gate of Detroit. They gained admittance as usual, but the soldiers were armed and ready for action.

On Monday they came again, to find the gates locked and barred. Major Gladwyn appeared, and said that while Pontiac himself might enter, he must leave his followers behind. Pontiac knew that his mask of friendship was no longer a disguise. He threw it off as he turned to his band. War was

ABOVE: A CLASSIC VIEW OF CHIEF PONTIAC HOLDING HIS BOW AND ARROWS. *OPPOSITE:* PONTIAC'S OTTAWA, POTAWATOMI, CHIPPEWA AND WYANDOT WARRIORS ATTACKED FORT DETROIT AT DAWN ON 7 MAY 1763.

declared. That night, in view of the fort, the campfires shone, and dawn brought a force of Ottawa, Potawatomi, Chippewa, and Wyandot against the fort. The attack was the harbinger of a general Native assault on the European outposts, and by June, Fort Pitt was also besieged.

The next month was filled with a series of minor attacks and depredations. The main forces of the Native Americans, however, were still so engaged upon the smaller forts and at Detroit that sufficient numbers could not be brought for a decisive onslaught. They could and did completely cut off communication with the settlements to the east. A truce was concluded at Detroit by October, though sporadic attacks continued.

In 1764, Colonel John Bradstreet took a force along the Great Lakes in an attempted counterattack. Described as a courageous blunderer, he satisfied himself with a nominal peace and a formal statement of allegiance. He was content with the bare assertion that those with whom he treated spoke for all the Native Americans of the West.

Pontiac maintained a vigorous siege of both the forts at Detroit and Pittsburgh for many months but, having no artillery, he was unable to carry them by assault. Nevertheless, he planned his efforts with skill. The experience of fighting with the French was put to good use.

Eventually the garrisons at both forts were relieved, and one by one, the peoples that Pontiac had rallied about him accepted a cessation of hostilities.

Pontiac had now, to his dismay, been told by French sources that the King of France would not return to retake his western empire. This he was reluctant to believe, but Pontiac agreed to discuss peace with Sir William Johnson.

'Friend, when the Great Father of France was in this country, I held him fast by the hand,' Pontiac told Johnson. 'Now that he is gone I take you, my English friend, by the hand, in the name of all the nations, and promise to keep this covenant as long as I shall live.'

Pontiac was killed in 1769, but he is remembered with pride by the warriors from the north who had thrilled to the Native American eloquence and exulted in the vaunting pride of their leader. Pontiac left his real imprint, not in Native American victory or defeat, but in the drawing together of the colonists.

RED JACKET

One of the most important figures among Native American leaders of the eighteenth century was Sogoyewapha, the fiery Seneca leader who was popularly known as Red Jacket because of a British officer's jacket that he often wore. He was a great personality and a powerful orator. He had convictions, ably defending his people and driving as hard a bargain as he could. He was a bitter rival of Chief Cornplanter because Red Jacket always advocated peace.

Though not inclined to war, he joined his people against the colonists in their rebellion against England in 1776. After the Revolutionary War, when the Iroquois and Algonquin people were encouraged by the Canadians to resist the United States and try to recover the Ohio Valley as British territory, Red Jacket appeared at Detroit with others to represent his people.

He was in favor of peace with the United States and supported his delegation in their refusal to be a party to the contemplated war with the United States. Ironically, Cornplanter also was there to throw his weight on the side of peace. Mohawk Chief Thayendanegea (known also as Joseph Brant) was thoroughly pro-British, but he could not prevail against the oratory of Red Jacket and the personality of Cornplanter.

During the War of 1812 most of the Six Nations of the Iroquois were loyal to the United States. After the Revolution, Cornplanter and Red Jacket stood consistently with the United States against all foes, Native American or European. Red Jacket joined the army in 1812 and participated in several important battles upon the Niagara frontier. The close of this war marked the end of Indian bloodshed in the Ohio and Michigan country, so that the problems confronting the Six Nations were those of peace.

Cornplanter was probably born between 1732 and 1740 and died in 1836, six years after Red Jacket's death. When the colonies revolted against the English, Cornplanter had led his people to war upon the settlements, but when the war was over he accepted the result and from then on was a powerful advocate for peace with the United States. Most of the treaties after 1784 bear his name. He was honored in life by the nation and by the state of Pennsylvania. Like Red Jacket, he met on occasion with President George Washington, General Anthony Wayne and other distinguished leaders of his time. He offered to lead a body of Seneca against the British in the War of 1812, but was not permitted only because of his advanced age. He was 56.

The many testimonials of his European contemporaries reveal that Cornplanter, like Red Jacket, was a man of uncommon personality, one of the great Native Americans of the time. An interesting insight into his character is conveyed by his request that his grave be not marked, so that it should be like those of his ancestors. Yet that was not to be, for neither Seneca nor American would respect so modest a request.

Unlike Cornplanter, Red Jacket was a an expansive politician. While Cornplanter hoped his grave would remain unmarked, Red Jacket, on his deathbed, reminded his family of his greatness, saying: 'When I am dead it will be noised abroad throughout the world. They will hear of it across the great waters and say, "Red Jacket the great orator is dead."'

Red Jacket's commentary on the spiritual beliefs of Native Americans (1805)

It was the will of the Great Spirit that we should meet together this day. He orders all things and has given us a fine day for our council. He has taken His garment from before the sun and caused it to shine with brightness upon us. Our eyes are opened that we see clearly, our ears are unstopped that we have been able to hear distinctly the words you have spoken. For all these favors we thank the Great Spirit, and Him only.

Brother, this council fire was kindled by you. It was at your request that we came together at this time. We have listened with attention to what you have said. You requested us to speak our minds freely. This gives us great joy, for we now consider that we stand upright before you and can speak what we think. All have heard your voice and all speak to you now as one man. Our minds are agreed.

Brother, you say you want an answer to your talk before you leave this place. It is right you should have one, as you are a great distance from home and we do not wish to detain you. But first we will look back a little and tell you what our fathers have told us and what we have heard from the white people.

Brother, listen to what we say. There was a time when our forefathers owned this great island. Their seats extended from the rising to the setting sun.

The Great Spirit had made it for the use of Indians. He had created the buffalo, the deer, and other animals for food. He had made the bear and the beaver. Their skins served us for clothing. He had scattered them over the country and taught us how to take them. He had caused the earth to produce corn for bread.

All this He had done for His red children because He loved them. If we had some disputes about our hunting-ground they were generally settled without the shedding of much blood.

But an evil day came upon us. Your forefathers crossed the great water and landed on this island. Their numbers were small. They found friends and not enemies.

They told us they had fled from their own country for fear of wicked men and had come here to enjoy their religion. They asked for a small seat. We took pity on them, granted their request, and they sat down among us. We gave them corn and meat, they gave us poison in return.

The white people, brother, had now found our country. Tidings were carried back and more came among us. Yet we did not fear them. We took them to be friends. They called us brothers. We believed them and gave them a larger seat. At length their numbers had greatly increased. They wanted more land, they wanted our country.

Our eyes were opened and our minds became uneasy. Wars took place. Indians were hired to fight against Indians, and many of our people were destroyed. They also brought strong liquor among us. It was strong and powerful, and has slain thousands.

Brother, our seats were once large and yours were small. You have now become a great people, and we have scarcely a place left to spread our blankets.

You have got our country, but are not satisfied. You want to force your religion upon us.

Brother, continue to listen. You say that you are sent to instruct us how to worship the Great Spirit agreeably to His mind, and, if we do not take hold of the religion which you white people teach we shall be unhappy hereafter. You say that you are right and we are lost.

How do we know this to be true? We understand that your religion is written in a Book. If it was intended for us, as well as you, why has not the Great Spirit given it to us, and not only to us, but why did He not give it to our forefathers the knowledge of that Book, with the means of understanding it rightly? We know only what you tell us about it. How shall we know when to believe, being so often deceived by the white people?

Brother, you say there is but one way to worship and serve the Great Spirit. If there is but one religion, why do you white people differ so much about it? Why not all agreed, as you can all read the Book?

Brother, we do not understand these things. We are told that your religion was

given to your forefathers and has been handed down from father to son. We also have a religion which was given to our forefathers and has been handed down to us, their children. We worship in that way. It teaches us to be thankful for all the favors we receive, to love each other, and to be united. We never quarrel about religion.

Brother, the Great Spirit has made us all, but He has made a great difference between His white and His Native children. He has given us different complexions and different customs. To you He has given the arts. To these He has not opened our eyes. We know these things to be true. Since He has made so great a difference between us in other things, why may we not conclude that He has given us a different religion according to our understanding?

The Great Spirit does right. He knows what is best for His children, we are satisfied.

Brother, we do not wish to destroy your religion or take it from you. We only want to enjoy our own.

Brother, you say you have not come to get our land or our money, but to enlighten our minds. I will now tell you that I

have been at your meetings and saw you collect money from the meeting. I cannot tell what this money was intended for, but suppose that it was for your minister, and, if we should conform to your way of thinking, perhaps you may want some from us.

Brother, we are told that you have been preaching to the white people in this place. These people are our neighbors. We are acquainted with them. We will wait a little while and see what effect your preaching has upon them. If we find it does them good, makes them honest, and less disposed to cheat Native Americans, we will then consider again of what you have said.

Brother, you have now heard our answer to your talk, and this is all we have to say at present. As we are going to part, we will come and take you by the hand, and hope the Great Spirit will protect you on your journey and return you safe to your friends.

JOSEPH BRANT

After Pontiac, few Native American military and political leaders of the eighteenth century match the towering stature of Mohawk Chief Thayendanegea (Joseph Brant). While Pontiac was the genius of the forest, Joseph Brant was the courtier and the diplomat. Pontiac favored guerrilla warfare. Brant took an English name and led his warriors as a division of the British Army and held the commission of a colonel in His Majesty's troops. Pontiac never embraced European customs, but Brant spent his declining years translating the New Testament into the Mohawk language. He died in 1807, at the age of 65.

His father was said to be a full-blood Mohawk. His mother may have been part European. He was born on the Ohio River, but he spent his boyhood in the Mohawk Valley, where his sister Molly, a year or two his senior, later became the wife of Sir William Johnson. Sir William's first wife was the niece of the powerful old Mohawk Chief Hendrick, and on her death, he married Molly Brant, or by some accounts they merely lived together. She apparently enjoyed all the position and influence that legal sanction might have given her.

In the shelter of Johnson Hall, and under the influence of his vigorous de facto brother-in-law, Joseph Brant grew to manhood. As a young man, he was a fighter, and was at the Crown Point Battle in 1755, when Hendrick aided William Johnson on his way to the career that led to his knighthood.

Joseph, as he liked to be called, attended the Wheelock School at Lebanon, Connecticut, the forerunner of Dartmouth College. He married and became a member of an Episcopal congregation. Brant not only learned the ways of the European, but he learned to follow them more faithfully in some respects than some Europeans.

In 1776, he went to Europe with Colonel Guy Johnson, Sir William's successor as superintendent of Indian affairs, and was by no means abashed in the presence of English courtiers and statesmen. Diplomatically he was triumphant. He surveyed the power and size of London, and decided that his fortunes would be cast with King George III. He promised Lord George Germain that the Six Nations would continue firm in their allegiance to the King.

He returned to America as Colonel Joseph Brant in the uniform of a British officer with his silver mounted cutlass and his shining silver epaulets. He would soon have occasion to use the cutlass.

In July of 1776, a certain famous Declaration had just been promulgated and the British would call upon the allegiance that he had pledged in London.

Both England and the colonies looked very dubiously upon the use of Native American warriors, but in the end used them. The visit of Brant and other leaders to England, on the eve of war, was part of a definite plan of rapprochement.

After the Americans defeated the British in the Revolution, Brant settled in Canada. There he dreamed of a great Native American state in the Ohio country with himself at its head, a result to be achieved by war, supported by the English, with the United States.

Between 1783 and 1790 the Native Americans of the Ohio country continued their warfare against the settlers. The Six Nations had taken no official part in this, as Cornplanter and Red Jacket, in opposition to Brant, did their best to maintain peace with the United States. In 1785 Brant toured the Ohio country, conferring with the Algonquin, urging them to unite against the United States and promising them the support of the British.

In 1784, Brant returned to England to seek an official promise of military aid for his scheme when the Native Americans went to war with the United States. Naturally he was refused, though it is doubtless that he was privately encouraged, as the British held the hope of all the Ohio country being recovered and added to Canada.

Upon his return Brant again sought to draw the Six Nations into the scheme, but Red Jacket and Cornplanter led the opposition as before. Nor was he more successful in attempting to organize the Ohio Algonquin, probably because those peoples had never submitted to a league or confederation like the Six Nations, and possibly because among them were the refugee Wyandot, who felt no particular desire to ally with the Iroquois.

Despite his efforts behind the scenes, Brant probably did not take an actual role in the Algonquin wars in the United States, and he died five years before the War of 1812.

Joseph Brant's London Address to Lord George Germain (1776)

We have crossed the great lake and come to this kingdom with our superintendent, Colonel Johnson, from our Confederacy of the Six Nations and their allies, that we might see our father, the great king, and join in informing him, his counselors, and wise men, of the good intentions of the Indians, our brothers, and of their attachment to his majesty and his government.

Brother, the disturbances in America give great trouble to all our nations, and many strange stories have been told to us by the people of that country. The Six Nations, who always loved the king, sent a number of their chiefs and warriors with their superintendent to Canada last summer, where they engaged their allies to join with them in the defense of that country, and when it was invaded by the New England people they alone defeated them.

Brother, in that engagement we had several of our best warriors killed and wounded, and the Indians think it very hard they should have been so deceived by the white people in that country, many returning in great numbers, and no white people supporting the Indians, they were obliged to return to their villages and wait.

We now, brother, hope to see these bad children chastised, and that we may be enabled to tell the Indians who have always been faithful and ready to assist the king what his majesty intends.

Brother, the Mohawks, our particular nation, have on all occasions shown their zeal and loyalty to the great king, yet they have been very badly treated by the people in that country, the city of Albany laying an unjust claim to the lands on which our lower castle is built, as George Klock and others do to those of Canajoharie, our upper village.

We have often been assured by our late great friend, Sir William Johnson, who never deceived us, and we know he was told so, that the king and wise men here would do us justice. But this, notwithstanding all our applications, has never been done, and it makes us very uneasy.

We also feel for the distress in which our brothers on the Susquehanna are likely to be involved by a mistake made in the boundary we settled in 1768.

This also our superintendent has laid before the king. We have only, therefore, to request that his majesty will attend to this matter: It troubles our nation and they can not sleep easy in their beds. Indeed, it is very hard, when we have let the king's subjects have so much land for so little value, they should want to cheat us in this manner of the small spots we have left for our women and children to live on.

We are tired out in making complaints and getting no redress. We therefore hope that the assurances now given us by the superintendent may take place and that he may have it in his power to procure us justice.

We will truly report all that we hear from you to the Six Nations on our return. We are well informed there have been many Indians in this country who came without any authority of their own and gave us much trouble.

We desire to tell you, brother, that this is not our case. We are warriors known to all the Nations, and are now here by approbation of many of them, whose sentiments we speak. Brother, we hope that these things will be considered and that the king or his great men will give us such answer as will make

ABOVE: THE GREAT IROQUOIS CHIEF THAYENDANEGEA, WHO TOOK THE NAME JOSEPH BRANT, IS REMEMBERED AS A GREAT STATESMAN AND DIPLOMAT.

our hearts light and glad before we go, and strengthen our hands, so that we may join our superintendent, Colonel Johnson, in giving satisfaction to all our Nations when we report to them on our return, for which purpose we hope soon to be accommodated with the passage.

TECUMSEH

In the early days of the nineteenth century, the settlers west of the Alleghenies were not present in sufficient numbers to seriously encroach upon the sovereignty of the Native Americans of the region. Ohio became a state in 1803, but her population was not large, and it was chiefly gathered along the Ohio River. The Territory of Indiana, the land beyond Ohio, of which General (later President) William Henry Harrison was military governor, was even more sparsely settled.

It is axiomatic that the white settlers did not understand the Native Americans. Seeing a people banded together, travelling together, sharing together the resources of food, the outsiders jumped to the conclusion that there was a common interest, that there was a fixed and formal government, the chief as a high magistrate with power to promulgate and enforce laws, and the warriors as a council whose word would be binding upon all the people. Believing in this interpretation, they made treaties and received plots of land. It was a theory the Native Americans had never accepted or even comprehended.

The treaties were made. With the Americans, the old policy which had been followed vaguely by Spanish and French and English became fixed by statute and decision. By American law, the government of the United States could acquire Native American lands, and that by cession from the government of the people. At Fort Wayne in 1809, Governor Harrison induced the Native Americans to cede three million acres. The frontier of the Americans had begun to move perilously near to the Shawnee villages on the Wabash River.

Among the Shawnee, the man who emerged as their most dynamic and respected leader was Tecumseh. He was a man of vision, power and persevering achievement. Also known as Tecumtha, he had seen much in his 40 years. His father had been killed in the Battle of Point Pleasant in 1774 when he was only six years old. An older brother, who seems to have been his mentor, fell in one of the border raids of the Revolutionary era.

Tecumseh had the gifts of courage and daring, and of intelligence and foresight as well. He had a plan which looked ahead, and he was willing to work steadily through the years to advance it. His ambition was no less than the federation of all the Native American peoples into a single state that could resist the advance of the Americans as a unit, and hold the Mississippi Valley forever.

He believed that no Indian chiefs had the right to dispose of the land by treaty. He went further, and declared that no whole people, even, had that right. The land belonged to all the peoples, to the people as a whole.

Tecumseh and his outspoken twin brother, Tenskwatawa, the shaman known to the white men as 'The Prophet,' told the Shawnee that they should go further and reject all the aspects of Euro-American culture, including such advances as metal tools and guns.

'Why do you suffer the Europeans to dwell among you?' Tecumseh asked. 'My children, you have forgotten the customs and traditions of your forefathers. Why do you not clothe yourselves in skins, as they did, and use the bows and arrows, and the stone-pointed lances, which they used? You have bought guns, knives, kettles, and blankets from the European, until you can no longer do without them, and what is worse, you have drunk the poison liquor which turns you into fools. Fling all these things away. Live as your wise forefathers lived before you.'

The Prophet preached that whites and Native Americans should remain separate. Native people should return to buckskin clothing and stone arrowheads, refuse the flesh of sheep and cattle and eat only of the meat of the wild creatures of the forest. Only those tools which they themselves could make and had invented, should be used. When they had learned to do all this the old happy days would dawn again.

Nearly a century later, in the excitement of the ghost dance, the vision was revisited by Wovoka.

William Henry Harrison had heard the message of The Prophet and he met with Tecumseh to discuss Shawnee concerns. After the meeting, he wrote of Tecumseh: 'He was one

of those uncommon geniuses which spring up occasionally to produce revolutions and overturn the established order of things. If it were not for the vicinity of the United States, he would perhaps be the founder of an empire that would rival in glory Mexico or Peru. No difficulties deter him. For four years he has been in constant motion. You see him today on the Wabash and in a short time hear of him on the shores of Lake Erie or Michigan, or on the banks of the Mississippi, and wherever he goes he makes an impression favorable to his purposes.'

In 1808, Tecumseh and The Prophet established a village at a site near the junction of the Tippecanoe and the Wabash rivers. From a strategic point of view it was an admirable choice as a center of either hostility or communication. Here The Prophet's power waxed ever larger and more powerful. The assembled Native Americans indulged in religious ceremonies and refused to buy ammunition from the traders, declaring that they could get all the arms and ammunition they needed without having to make any payment for it.

By a treaty entered into at Fort Wayne in 1809, Governor Harrison had obtained cession of the Indian land east of the Wabash. He had bidden to the council all the peoples that could claim any interest whatever in the lands to which he sought to extinguish the Native American title. But on Tecumseh's theory it would have been necessary, to make the transfer binding, to gain the consent of every people and each individual member.

The following year Tecumseh and 400 warriors swept down the Wabash in their canoes to confer with Governor Harrison at Vincennes. Tecumseh's professed purpose was to assure the Governor that he had not allied himself with the British forces in the war which all felt now to be imminent. His actual discourse was an eloquent recital of the wrongs of his people, and of the succession of treaties which had year by year diminished their lands and deprived them of their hunting grounds. He ended with an appeal that the treaty of Fort Wayne be set aside. Governor Harrison promised to report his request to Washington.

Tecumseh replied, 'As the great chief [in Washington] is to determine the matter, I hope the Great Spirit will put sense enough into his head to induce him to give up this land. It is true, he is so far off he will not be injured by this war, he may sit still in his town and drink his wine whilst you and I will have to fight it out.'

ABOVE: A CLASSIC PORTRAIT OF TECUMSEH IN THE UNIFORM OF AN AMERICAN BRIGADIER GENERAL. *OPPOSITE:* THE BATTLE OF TIPPECANOE, FOUGHT IN NOVEMBER 1811, INVOLVED INTENSE HAND-TO-HAND COMBAT.

Tecumseh had brought all the northern peoples into his confederation, and his next step would be to unite the southern bands with them. A few days after this council at Vincennes, Tecumseh went to visit the Creek and the Choctaw. Of the results of that visit we shall have ample evidence in the later story of the southern conflicts.

Tecumseh had told his followers to keep the peace during his absence and to make ready for the great day when the signal should go forth for all the peoples at one moment to take up the cause.

'Do you not believe that the Great Spirit has sent me?' he asked the Creeks at Tuckhabatchee. 'You shall know. I leave

Tuckhabatchee directly and shall go straight to Detroit. When I arrive there, I shall stamp on the ground with my foot and shake down every house in Tuckhabatchee.'

By sheer coincidence, an earthquake shook the lower Mississippi region and shattered the huts of Tuckhabatchee about the time the watching Creek thought he must have reached Detroit. However, Tecumseh came back to find that things had not gone so well in the North. His guiding hand removed, the warriors had enjoyed all too well their raiding upon the border farms and settlements. Governor Harrison felt that the safety of his people required him to demand that the Native Americans give up those among them who had been active in the murder of European families. He sent messages to all the peoples urging them to remain friendly to the United States. The Prophet countered with his own messages, urging them to stand firm against the intruders.

To the Delaware, who had remained friendly to the settlers, The Prophet announced that they must make a decision between them at once. They went to him counselling peace, but returned to tell of the insult with which they had been received. Governor Harrison sent a delegation of Miami on a similar errand. They listened and remained with The Prophet. Evidently they believed his great town would prevail against the scattered settlers.

Governor Harrison decided on a show of force, and in October 1811, he led a force toward the headquarters of The Prophet on the banks of the Tippecanoe. The Prophet proposed a council and Harrison agreed — though without much belief in the sincerity of the proposal. On 6 November, the night was moonless and rainy. At four o'clock a sentinel saw the foremost of a line of warriors who had stealthily encircled the

camp. His shot called the soldiers into action. The battle was short, and the forces rallied by The Prophet were defeated.

Tecumseh returned from the South to find the Prophet's town deserted and his hope of an Indian federation in ruin. Having had his forces defeated by the Americans, Tecumseh turned to the British, offered an exchange of services, and was made an officer in the Army of King George.

'Tecumseh was very prepossessing,' wrote a British officer who was present when the Native American leader joined his forces with those of the King. 'His figure was light and finely proportioned, his height five feet nine or ten inches, his complexion light copper, his countenance oval, with bright hazel eyes beaming cheerfulness, energy, and decision. Three small crowns or coronets were suspended from the lower cartilage of his aquiline nose, and a large silver medallion of George the Third, which I believe his ancestor had received from Lord Dorchester when Governor General of Canada, was attached to a mixed colored string which hung around his neck.'

Tecumseh was made master of all the Native American troops — including even the Sioux — that were allied with the British, though each band had its own chiefs. Their first success at Brownsville was to his credit, and after a year of warfare Tecumseh was a tower of strength to his allies. General Sir Isaac Brock wrote: 'The conduct of the Indians, joined to that of the gallant and brave chiefs of their respective peoples, has since the commencement of the war been marked with acts of true heroism.' Brock also gave Tecumseh much of the credit

---

BELOW: THE BATTLE OF THE THAMES ON 5 OCTOBER 1813. *OPPOSITE:* TECUMSEH'S TWIN BROTHER, THE SHAMAN TENSKWATAWA, WHO WAS GENERALLY KNOWN TO NON-NATIVES AS THE PROPHET.

for the British success at Detroit, and in recognition of his aid, Brock decorated Tecumseh with his own sash and pistols.

By 1813, however, Tecumseh's Native American/British military alliance had begun to crumble. Native American interest in the War of 1812 had been waning as British power seemed to wane. Before this the lower peoples had wished to go back to their own land and assure the Americans of their neutrality. Tecumseh himself had all but made up his mind to leave but had been dissuaded by the persuasions of the Sioux and the Chippewa — old foes who found themselves for the first time on the same side of a conflict.

General Henry Proctor, who succeeded Brock after the latter's death, had the dubious task of being in charge when the British forces began to collapse. But Tecumseh wished to fight in earnest and he did not relish Proctor's idea of retreat.

'You are like a fat dog,' he told Proctor, 'that carries his tail on his back, but when frightened, drops it between his legs and runs off.'

The British general felt that the endurance of insolence and abuse was a high price to pay for the Native American alliance. Not all Tecumseh's eloquence could induce him to make a stand. Finally, on the Thames, they made a stand, albeit against the odds. Their opponent was none other than William Henry Harrison.

Tecumseh went into the fight on the morning of the fifth of October 1813, with the conviction that it would be his last. He was right. For a while, his voice was heard above the din of battle, urging on his men, but when that voice was heard no more, the Native Americans scattered and the British gave up.

Tecumseh was gone, and gone was the hope of Native American unity in the region. The British government pensioned his family and the Prince Regent sent his 17-year-old son a sword, but Tecumseh's dream of a great Indian nation had faded away even as his voice died out that day upon the Thames.

Tecumseh had looked back upon earlier Native American triumphs. He believed that the English of Canada would not only support his Indian state but would respect its borders. He did not see that the English friendliness in Canada was little more than intrigue and that the English interest lay in stirring up the Native Americans to check the advance of the United States, in order to leave the way open for their own expansion.

Tecumseh had believed the Native Americans powerful enough to win against the United States, if they would unite under one leadership, and he stood to offer that leadership. Ultimately he died in battle, a noble death for a noble chief with a grand vision for his people.

The Prophet lived for a quarter of a century after the Thames, no doubt reflecting upon Tippecanoe and the collapse of his and his brothers' dreams. There is a story that he put a curse on Harrison for the defeats at Tippecanoe and the Thames. Elected president of the United States in 1840, Harrison died after only a month in office. In what is known as the 'Zero Year Curse,' every man elected president in 20 year increments from 1840 through 1960 *also* died in office.

Tecumseh's address, delivered to William Henry Harrison at Vincennes (1810)

I am a Shawnee. My forefathers were warriors. Their son is a warrior. From them I take only my existence, from my people I take nothing. I am the maker of my own fortune, and oh! that I could make that of my Native people, and of my country, as great as the conceptions of my mind, when I think of the Spirit that rules the universe. I would not then come to Governor Harrison to ask him to tear the treaty and to obliterate the landmark, but I would say to him: 'Sir, you have liberty to return to your own country.'

The being within, communing with past ages, tells me that once, nor until lately, there was no white man on this continent, that it then all belonged to Native men, children of the same parents, placed on it by the Great Spirit that made them, to keep it, to traverse it, to enjoy its productions, and to fill it with the same race, once a happy race, since made miserable by the white people, who have never contented but are always encroaching. The way, and the only way, to check and to stop this evil, is for all the Native men to unite in claiming a common and equal right in the land, as it was at first, and should be yet, for it never was divided, but belongs to all for the use of each.

For no part has a right to sell, even to each other, much less to strangers, those who want all, and will not do with less.

The white people have no right to take the land from the Native Americans, because they had it first, it is theirs. They may sell, but all must join. Any sale not made by all is not valid. The late sale is bad. It was made by a part only. Part do not know how to sell. It requires all to make a bargain for all.

All Native men have equal rights to the unoccupied land. The right of occupancy is as good in one place as in another. There cannot be two occupations in the same place. The first excludes all others.

It is not so in hunting or travelling, for there the same ground will serve many, as they may follow each other all day, but the camp is stationary, and that is occupancy. It belongs to the first who sits down on his blanket or skins which he has thrown upon the ground, and till he leaves it no other has a right.

Tecumseh's address to General Proctor (1813)

Sir, listen to us. We are all before you. The war before this, our British father gave the hatchet to his Native children when old chiefs were alive. They are now dead. In that war our father was thrown on his back by the Americans, and our father took them by the hand without our knowledge, and we are afraid that our father will do so again at this time.

Summer before last, when I came forward with my red brethren and was ready to take up the hatchet in favor of our British father, we were told not to be in a hurry, that he had not yet determined to fight the Americans.

Listen! When war was declared, our father stood up and gave us the tomahawk, and told us that he was ready to strike the Americans, that he wanted our assistance, and that he would certainly get us our lands back, which the Americans had taken from us.

Listen! You told us at that time to bring forward our families to this place, and we did so, and you promised to take care of them, and that they should want for nothing while the men would go and fight the enemy. That we need not trouble ourselves about the enemy's garrisons, that we knew nothing about them, and that our father would attend to that part of the business. You also told your Native American children that you would take good care of your garrison here, which made our hearts glad.

Listen! When we were last at the Rapids, it is true that we gave you little assistance. It is hard to fight people who live like ground hogs.

Listen! Our fleet has gone out, we know they have fought, we have heard the great guns, but know nothing of what has happened to our father with one arm. Our ships have gone one way, and we are much astonished to see our father tying up everything and preparing to run away the other, without letting

his Native children know what his intentions are. You always told us to remain here and take care of our lands. It made our hearts glad to hear that was your wish.

Our great father, the king, is the head, and you represent him. You always told us that you would never draw your foot off British ground, but now, father, we see you are drawing back, and we are sorry to see our father doing so without seeing the enemy. We must compare our father's conduct to a fat animal that carries its tail upon its back, but when frightened it drops it between its legs and runs off.

Listen, father! The Americans have not yet defeated us by land, neither are we sure that they have done so by water. We therefore wish to remain here and fight our enemy should they make their appearance. If they defeat us, we will then retreat with our father.

At the Battle of the Rapids, last war, the Americans certainly defeated us, and when we retreated to our father's fort in that place the gates were shut against us. We were afraid that it would now be the case, but instead of that we now see our British father preparing to march out of his garrison.

ABOVE: WHEN TECUMSEH WAS KILLED IN THE BATTLE OF THE THAMES, HIS BROTHER IS SAID TO HAVE PUT A CURSE ON WILLIAM HENRY HARRISON, WHO DIED ONE MONTH AFTER BECOMING PRESIDENT OF THE UNITED STATES.

Father! You have got the arms and ammunition which our great father sent for his Native children. If you have an idea of going away, give them to us, and you may go and welcome. For us, our lives are in the hands of the Great Spirit. We are determined to defend our lands, and if it is His will we wish to leave our bones upon them.

OSCEOLA

It can be said with certainty that the region west of the Alleghenies and Appalachians was only sparsely settled by whites in the early days of the nineteenth century. Until the time of Tippecanoe (1811), the settlers that were present did not seriously encroach upon the Native Americans who had lived there for centuries. After the Creek War of 1813-1814, the First Seminole War of 1816, and certainly by the 1820s, this had changed dramatically.

By the end of the 1820s, Americans considered settlement west of the Alleghenies and Appalachians to be their manifest destiny. If they could not live in harmony with the Native Americans, then they would get rid of the Indians. It was their birthright to displace people that had been born in the area for generations. President Andrew Jackson, a no-nonsense war hero, came to office in 1829 with a plan to simply move the Native Americans west of the Mississippi River into what is now Oklahoma.

The Indian Removal Act of 1830 stands as one of the most abhorrent pieces of legislation ever passed by the United States Congress. By 1832 the removal policy of the government had been carried out almost everywhere. The Creek were nearly gone and it was supposed that the related Seminole peoples of Florida would be willing to travel with them to the new land.

The Treaty of Payne's Landing was negotiated on this basis.

The Seminole were to cede to the United States their Florida lands, and receive in return a portion of the Creek territory in the west. The emigration was to take place within three years, beginning in 1833, but the United States Senate was slow to confirm the treaty, and it was not proclaimed as law until 12 April 1834, more than a year after the Seminole were supposed to start moving.

Meanwhile, Seminole Chief Mickenopah (Micanopy) had refused to sign the Treaty of Payne's Landing, or rather by remaining away from the meeting had permitted his leadership to pass into the hands of those who were not unwilling to sign. He was a proud leader. What he really wanted was to remain on his fertile acres surrounded by his hundred African slaves.

After 1834, Mickenopah aligned himself with the younger warriors who were strong in opposition to the treaty and the move. They were ready to go to war. Most of the Seminole were now refusing to go. The stalemate continued to 1835, and it was apparent that the Seminole would not leave Florida unless forced.

As usually happens in times such as this, a leader emerged in the moment of his peoples' need. In this case, it was the 30-year-old Chief Osceola. His name was derived from a word meaning 'the rising sun.'

A dramatic story of the times represents Osceola as attending a meeting at which the chiefs were urged to sign a paper acknowledging the validity of the agreement to migrate. A few were prevailed upon to do so, but Osceola, rising from his place, walked forward to the table where the document lay. Drawing his long knife, he raised it far above his head for a moment, and then brought it down vigorously, piercing the paper and sinking it deep into the wood beneath.

'This,' he exclaimed 'is the only way I will sign!'

OPPOSITE: A LITHOGRAPH OF THE SEMINOLE CHIEF OSCEOLA. *BELOW:* THE GREAT CHIEF MICKENOPAH REFUSED TO ACCEPT THE IDEA THAT THE SEMINOLE SHOULD BE EVICTED AS THE CREEK HAD BEEN.

stepped away from the meeting, returned to Emaltha and shot him.

In December, US Army troops had arrived to enforce the removal treaty, though as yet they had taken no steps that looked toward fighting. Osceola, now risen to be war leader, proved himself not unskilled in strategy. The women and children were sent deep into the swamps. The cattle and hogs were driven into secret hiding places in the Everglades to which Europeans had never penetrated. Supplies and weapons of all sorts were ready.

On 28 December open warfare began. Major Francis Dade and his command started north from Fort Brooke, on Tampa Bay, to reinforce Fort King. Marching through the sparse pine woods, they were suddenly fired upon from all sides. Mickenopah and his attacking Seminoles were well hidden, and after an hour of fighting, it became apparent that Dade's troops could not go on, as the wounded were now too many to carry. It

The meeting broke up in confusion. Osceola was detained as a prisoner for four days and released. The army had failed to recognize a declaration of war.

The Second Seminole War began in November 1835 with an attack upon Charley Emaltha, one of the treaty-signing chiefs. Emaltha wished to carry out his agreement, and with a band of followers was making preparations for the westward journey. Pressed by Osceola and a group of warriors for a decision, Emaltha refused to change his purpose. Osceola raised his rifle to kill the chief. Abraham, an African interpreter that was a slave to Mickenopah, intervened and suggested a council. So the Seminole retired to consider the matter. Osceola

was impossible either to advance or to retreat. Major Dade had fallen early in the action, and most of the men were dead or dying. It was nearly two months before General Gaines and his volunteers from New Orleans reached the spot and buried the victims of this first battle of the war.

The Seminoles remained secure in their traditional lands for several months, but soon Osceola came face to face with a new and bitter foe. General Thomas Jesup succeeded to the

OPPOSITE: THE ARREST OF CHIEF OSCEOLA AT FORT MELLON. *ABOVE:* FOLLOWING IN OSCEOLA'S FOOTSTEPS, CHIEF BILLY BOWLEGS LED THE RESISTANCE DURING THE SEMINOLE WAR OF 1856-1858. HE DIED IN 1863 OR 1864.

command of the forces which were a combination of regular troops and Florida volunteers.

In May 1836, Osceola came in to Fort Mellon with a considerable party and used an elaborate ruse to trick the army out of a large quantity of supplies, and buy time. The general reflected that the trick had proved an excellent means of recuperation for the enemy. In October he came in, again under a white flag, to Saint Augustine. General Jesup gave his men orders to surround them, and the entire group, 72 warriors and six women, were quietly taken prisoner. The old Spanish dungeons of Fort Marion were conveniently at hand, and the Seminole were thrown into them. This capture of civilians under a white flag roused a storm of protest which was to haunt General Jesup for the remainder of his life.

He had violated international law, and committed an act of treachery which nothing could palliate. Nothing could or would ever do justice to his misdeed.

'Never,' implored a London magazine, 'was a more disgraceful piece of villainy perpetrated in a civilized land.'

Even the public outcry could not free the brave and proud Osceola. Early in 1837, he was transferred with his fellow warriors to Sullivan's Island, opposite Charleston, South Carolina. He became the hero of the day. Visitors thronged to the island to see the chief and talk with him.

When he and a party of braves visited the theater in Charleston, they vied with the actors in holding the attention and admiration of the audience. It was while he was incarcerated at Fort Moultrie that Osceola was visited by George Catlin, the great portrait artist, fresh from the painting of Keokuk, Black Hawk, and Sauk notables.

Catlin was eager to add to his portfolio of Seminole chiefs before they were sent to Oklahoma. For Catlin, Osceola arrayed himself in his best and stood, accoutred for war, while the painting was done.

OPPOSITE: THE CLASSIC IMAGE OF OSCEOLA IS GEORGE CATLIN'S GREAT PORTRAIT, PAINTED AT SULLIVAN'S ISLAND, SOUTH CAROLINA IN 1837. *BELOW:* AN 1860 ENGRAVING OF THE BATTLE OF OKEECHOBEE, ON 25 DECEMBER 1837, IN THE FLORIDA EVERGLADES.

'I have painted him,' wrote the artist, 'in precisely the costume in which he stood for his picture, even to a string and a trinket. He wore three ostrich feathers in his head and a turban made of a varicolored cotton shawl, and his dress was chiefly of calicoes, with a handsome bead sash or belt around his waist, and his rifle in his hand.'

Osceola is seen as a rather fine looking young man as Catlin has delineated him for us. The older Mickenopah wanted to present himself properly, and he wore a pair of red leggings of which he was particularly proud. The artist obliged him by a portrait in which the old chief sits cross-legged, bedecked with bows, beaded, with a rose-tinted mantle as large as a bedspread draped about one shoulder.

Neither of these men was to see the western lands to which the Seminoles were to be sent. Mickenopah died on the way, and Osceola before they were to have left. Shortly after his portrait was finished he became ill with 'a quinsy or putrid sore throat,' as the artist records it.

Doctors were sent from Charleston to care for him, but he refused them, preferring traditional medicine. It was too late for either. A half hour before his death he called for his costumes of war and donned them. At his request the officers of the post were summoned to see him arrayed for battle.

Before their gaze he painted one side of his face with vermilion as one going into the fight. In silence, he shook hands with all the onlookers, let himself be lowered again upon his bed and drew his knife. Grasping it in his right hand he folded his arms across his breast, and so, without a struggle, died.

BLACK HAWK and KEOKUK

The Sauk (Sac) people were known to be living in Michigan and Wisconsin during the eighteenth century, but with the arrival of the European settlers, they gradually migrated westward, across the Mississippi to what is now Iowa and Oklahoma.

The Sauk, often called Sac, a French interpretation of the word, are generally associated with the Mesquaki (Muskwaki) people, who are known as the Fox. Indeed, in general usage, the names are coupled as Sauk & Fox, and the two peoples were traditionally almost identical in language.

Two of the most important leaders among the Sauk & Fox peoples were the Sauk chiefs Black Hawk, born in 1767, and Keokuk, born in about 1790, although some sources indicate that he may have been born as early as 1770. The two men could hardly have been more different in political outlook. Black Hawk was staunchly opposed to détente with the settlers, while Keokuk had other ambitions. He longed to become a great peace leader and an orator.

The Sauk people had aided Pontiac in his great struggle in the 1772 to 1776 period, and doubtless the tales of this war fired the imagination of the young Black Hawk. As his sympathies were with the English, he took part in the War of 1812 and served with Tecumseh, whose sympathies were decidedly anti-American.

Keokuk, on the other hand, was friendly to the United States, though he did not take up arms in their support. He was a liberal in that he favored changing old customs and adopting some features of European civilization when such innovations seemed advantageous.

After the War of 1812, European settlement proceeded rapidly westward, encroaching upon the Sauk & Fox, who in fact sold some of their lands. Keokuk favored the sales and the accompanying treaties, but Black Hawk always opposed such agreements. He led what may be called the radical and militant wing of the people. Black Hawk, following in the footsteps of King Metacomet, Pontiac, Tecumseh and others, sought to federate the Native Americans to resist the Europeans.

In 1832, Black Hawk repudiated the sale of Sauk lands east of the Mississippi and declared war on the settlers. Keokuk remained neutral in what was to be known as the Black Hawk War.

For generations of Americans, both Native Americans and Americans of European ancestry, the name Black Hawk was familiar on many levels. Not the least of these involved the Black Hawk War, a conflict in which Abraham Lincoln served as a soldier.

The war was in fact a succession of running battles in which Black Hawk showed great courage and skill as a leader. After many early victories, the tide turned against Black Hawk. His forces were defeated in July and August by General Dodge and General Atkinson in battles on the Wisconsin and Bad Axe Rivers, and he was forced to surrender to General Street at Prairie du Chien on 27 August 1832.

He was placed in the custody of a young US Army lieutenant named Jefferson Davis. This was, of course, the same Jefferson Davis who would become president of the Confederate States of America in 1861. By curious coincidence or irony, Robert Anderson, who commanded Fort Sumter in 1861, along with Abraham Lincoln, were also serving at this time against Black Hawk. Also curious is that Black Hawk, on being taken to the East as a prisoner of war, was confined at Fort Monroe, Louisiana, where, 33 years later, Jefferson Davis was incarcerated as a defeated leader of his people.

Before going to Fort Monroe, Black Hawk was taken to Washington and presented to Andrew Jackson at the White House, where Black Hawk told the president 'I am a man and you are another.'

After the tension was relieved and hostilities had cooled, Black Hawk was allowed to return to Iowa. In the meantime, Andrew Jackson had recognized Keokuk, and Keokuk was made head chief. Legend has it that Black Hawk so resented this that he removed his breechcloth and struck Keokuk in the face with it.

ABOVE: BLACK HAWK, WHOSE NATIVE NAME WAS MUCKATAHMISHOKAHKAIK, WAS A GIFTED ORATOR. *OPPOSITE:* THE GREAT SAUK CHIEF KEOKUK, OR WATCHFUL FOX, PHOTOGRAPHED IN 1847 BY THOMAS M EASTERLY.

When Black Hawk died in 1838, Lorado Taft, a distinguished sculptor of the day, executed a heroic statue of this celebrated chief, which was erected on the banks of Rock River near Oregon, in northern Illinois.

Keokuk's greatest achievement was his appearance in Washington as an advocate for his people, and to contest the claim of the Sioux to lands occupied by the Sauk & Fox. Here, his great oratorical powers were shown at their best. His logic and command of the facts were also above adverse criticism. In short, he won his case.

He went on to tour the important cities of the nation, where great honors were showered upon him. He died in 1848, and in 1883 his bones were moved to Keokuk, Iowa, a city named in his honor, and interred with great solemnity. A large monument was set up to perpetuate his memory, and there is also a bronze bust of him in the Capitol at Washington.

Keokuk was a man of truly great wisdom, who had the gift of speech, who understood the importance of diplomacy, yet demanded justice from the Europeans and the right to live in peace among them.

Black Hawk's Surrender Address (1832)

You have taken me prisoner, with all my warriors. I am much grieved, for I expected, if I did not defeat you, to hold out much longer, and give you more trouble, before I surrendered. I tried hard to bring you into ambush, but your last general understood Indian fighting. I determined to rush on you, and fight you face to face. I fought hard. But your guns were well aimed. The bullets flew like birds in the air, and whizzed by our ears like the wind through the trees in winter. My warriors fell around me. It began to look dismal.

I saw my evil day at hand. The sun rose dim on us in the morning, and at night it sank in a dark cloud, and looked like a ball of fire. That was the last sun that shone on Black Hawk. His heart is dead, and no longer beats quick in his bosom. He is now a prisoner of the white men, they will do with him as they wish. But he can stand torture, and is not afraid of death. He is no coward. Black Hawk is an Indian. He has done nothing for which an Indian ought to be ashamed. He has fought for his countrymen, against white men, who came, year after year, to cheat them and take away their lands.

The white men despise the Indians, and drive them from their homes. They smile in the face of the poor Indian, to cheat him, they shake him by the hand, to gain his confidence, to make him drunk, and to deceive him. We told them to let us alone, and keep away from us, but they followed on and beset our paths, and they coiled themselves among us like the snake. They poisoned us by their touch. We were not safe. We lived in danger.

We looked up to the Great Spirit. We went to our father. We were encouraged. His great council gave us fair words and big promises, but we got no satisfaction: things were growing worse. There were no deer in the forest. The opossum and beaver were fled. The springs were drying up, and our squaws and papooses were without food to keep them from starving.

We called a great council and built a large fire. The spirit of our fathers arose, and spoke to us to avenge our wrongs or die. We set up the war-whoop, and dug up the tomahawk, our knives were ready, and the heart of Black Hawk swelled high in his bosom, when he led his warriors to battle.

He is satisfied. He will go to the world of spirits contented. He has done his duty. His father will meet him there, and commend him.

Black Hawk is a true Indian, and disdains to cry like a woman. He feels for his wife, his children, and his friends. But he does not care for himself. He cares for the Nation and the Indians. They will suffer. He laments their fate.

Farewell, my Nation! Black Hawk tried to save you, and avenge your wrongs. He drank the blood of some of the whites. He has been taken prisoner, and his plans are crushed. He can do no more. He is near his end. His sun is setting, and he will rise no more. Farewell to Black Hawk!

BELOW: KEOKUK IN AN 1835 PAINTING BY GEORGE CATLIN. *OPPOSITE:* A PORTRAIT OF CHIEF BLACK HAWK.

RED CLOUD

Today, when we think of glorious halcyon days of Native Americans as a free and independent people, it is in the detached context of the distant past. It was an era that existed before our grandparents' time. However, in the early twentieth century, as automobiles, and telephones were coming to be part of the daily lives of most Americans, those glory days were still part of the conscious memory of many people. When people of that era thought about the great Native leaders of recent memory, one name always came to the forefront.

Makhpiyaluta, or Red Cloud, was generally remembered by all Americans as 'the greatest Indian of modern times.'

He belonged to the Oglala division of Teton Sioux. He was born in about 1822 at the forks of the Platte River and died at Pine Ridge, South Dakota. It is said that he counted coups — that is, he touched the bodies of enemies — 80 times with his coup-stick.

He first came to prominence in 1865, when the US Government undertook to build a road from Fort Laramie, Wyoming to the gold fields of Montana. Red Cloud captured a detachment of troops, held them for two weeks, and released them without injury. Commissioners were sent out from Washington that autumn to negotiate his cooperation in the road construction project, but he refused to meet with them.

Of the individuals who exerted an influence upon the various bands of Sioux, perhaps Sitting Bull and Red Cloud are more popularly known than others. Army officers stationed on the frontier in the 1860s or 1870s testified to their courage. War Department records contain more frequent mention of Red Cloud than of any other Native leaders.

The ethnographer C W Allen, who was well acquainted with Red Cloud, prepared an oral history before the chief's memory failed, and much of what we know from other sources has been corroborated. We know that Red Cloud was born in 1822, a year that a particularly large meteor was observed over the plains. In Sioux legend it was 'Star-passed-by-with-a-loud-noise winter.' The Sioux designated each year by some particular or striking occurrence. For instance, in Red Cloud's 'winter counts,' or census, one winter is called 'Winter-in-which-many-died-of-smallpox,' and another, 'Winter-we-killed-one-hundred-white-men.'

Little is known of Red Cloud's earlier days. When asked in the early twentieth century, he shrugged his shoulders and said, 'All great men were once boys.'

All Native American children learned to ride when extremely young. General Grenville Dodge wrote that, whether men or boys, the Plains peoples, or, as some Army officers called them, 'Horse Indians,' produced the finest horsemen in the world.

Red Cloud was not a hereditary chief, but arose to this position through merit. He was about 16 when he became a leader among the other boys, distinguishing himself in skirmishes and battles with the Crow, Pawnee, and other hereditary enemies of the Sioux. The various winter counts tell of serious battles between the Crow and the Sioux. Between 1840 and 1849 there were few attacks against settlers on the Plains, and most of these occurred to the south, in Texas, or along the old Santa Fe Trail.

It was not until 1849, in the wake of the discovery of gold, that extensive emigration began toward California. As the wagon trains increased, the hunting of the Native Americans was seriously interfered with. Expeditions, not only of United States troops but of adventurers, buffalo hunters, and miners, penetrated to various parts of the West. Among these travellers were people with low regard for the Native American. They fired on peaceful parties of hunting Indians without the slightest provocation.

Wagon trains were often led by men from the East who knew nothing whatsoever of Native Americans or their habits, and becoming frightened at the approach of either friendly or hostile Native Americans, opened fire without the slightest thought of consequences. It is therefore not surprising that all the Plains Native Americans soon assumed a hostile attitude toward any and all of the intruders.

Meanwhile, the buffalo were being hunted more heavily, and eventually to the brink of extinction. In oral histories undertaken early in the twentieth century, many of the Plains people agreed that the destruction of the buffalo was the greatest calamity ever brought upon them. They could forgive the whites for attacking their villages, for the disregard of treaty promises, and overlook the seizure of their lands, but they could not forget that the Americans made useless and unnecessary slaughter of that grand, majestic native animal, typical of the 'spirit of the Plains.'

Today it is hard to imagine what the buffalo meant to the Native American. Thousands of men flocked west to hunt buffalo solely for their hides. Most of them were inexperienced and destroyed many animals before they learned how to properly prepare a robe for sale. The great Platte, the Arkansas, the Nebraska and other Plains rivers, were in a few years lined with millions of skeletons — a pitiful spectacle — wretched relics of a once noble creature.

Complaints were made by the Native Americans, who depended solely upon the buffalo for existence, to the government at Washington, but without avail. More butchers, attracted by the alluring and exciting life of the hunter, flocked to the West. They strained every nerve to make a 'record' in destroying these animals. To be a buffalo-hunter became popular, and a number of persons have since carried through life names distinguishing them from their fellows because of the exceeding slaughter which they made.

Colonel H I Dodge, the author of several books and treatises on Native Americans, and who spent from 1849 to 1884 on the frontier, blamed the hunters, miners, and cowboys for the

---

OPPOSITE: THE CLASSIC RED CLOUD PORTRAIT, PHOTOGRAPHED BY CHARLES BELL IN 1880 DURING THE CHIEF'S VISIT TO WASHINGTON, DC.

warfare that took place in the West. Dodge felt that these people regarded the rights of no persons, save themselves. The government, meanwhile, did little but send Peace Commissions and armies in rotation.

The Sioux held a great council, which was attended by the dissatisfied among other groups, and decided to drive out all the whites found in their hunting territory. They split up into small bands, attacked emigrant trains, killed hunters, and at the time of the Civil War (1861-1865) were carrying on a general warfare from the Black Hills of South Dakota to the frontiers of Texas.

After the terrible wars of 1862 in Minnesota, the Native Americans became bolder, and having received recruits from the bands who had fled from Minnesota, they held up several large wagon trains, killed or captured the escorts and appropriated the goods. When the news of this affair reached Washington, Colonels Henry Carrington and William Fetterman were ordered to subdue the Plains Indians, and were sent to Wyoming, where they established Fort Phil Kearny on the Piney Fork of the Powder River.

Not only was this movement necessary on the part of the government because of the hostility of the Sioux, but it was desired to open a road through the Powder River country to Virginia City and other mining towns in the mountains of Montana, and also to Oregon.

Part of the territory was owned by the Crow, but the Dakota had usurped most of it as hunting grounds for themselves. Several conferences between the authorities and the Native Americans were held, but dissatisfaction among the Native Americans was such that no settlement could be effected. 'We will lose,' said they, 'all our best hunting territory if this route is established.'

Red Cloud and other chiefs, such as Crazy Horse and American Horse, saw the necessity for open hostilities. During the ensuing struggle Red Cloud would win a great reputation as a leader.

During these troubled times, Fort Laramie was the center of important conferences between the Native Americans and the army. Red Cloud presented a striking figure at the Fort Laramie assembly in the spring of 1866. He arrived with the same party of Sioux and Cheyenne warriors with whom he had earlier held up the construction workers sent to begin the Powder River Road. On this matter of a road he would not retreat. Now in council, tall, eloquent, determined, he repeated

his refusal to let the intruder make a way across his hunting grounds.

As the council talk went on, General Carrington approached with his troops, assuming that the Sioux would consent and that they might go on to open the way and to establish the forts for the protection of the road. Red Cloud's anger flamed into action. At his word, his followers mounted up and rode away. Red Cloud's shout of angry defiance rang in the ears of the councilors.

In August, the army began building Fort Phil Kearny. For the next two years, every day the lookout would scan the hills and signal the approach of Native Americans or more soldiers. Not a message went down the trail to Laramie, not a mail or

supply train came up from Nebraska, without meeting the deadly opposition of Red Cloud and his warriors. Not even the cold of the northern winter could relax his determination.

When Colonel Carrington and his troops left Laramie in June 1866, they were constantly watched by Red Cloud.

With these troops was Captain Frederick Brown, noted for his bravery, but also for his contempt of Native Americans. Both officers declared that 'a nervy white could put to flight a hundred Sioux.'

When calling one evening, Brown told Colonel Carrington's wife that he would have Red Cloud's scalp before he returned East. The prophecy would not be fulfilled. Instead, it was Brown who lost his.

ABOVE: THE BRUTAL MASSACRE OF NATIVE AMERICANS BY US ARMY TROOPS AT SAND CREEK, COLORADO IN NOVEMBER 1864 INITIATED A MOOD OF ILL WILL ON THE PLAINS THAT WOULD LAST FOR A GENERATION.

Meanwhile, Red Cloud harassed the garrison of Fort Phil Kearny constantly, killing small parties of wood-cutters, and it became necessary to send out a guard of fifty to eighty men with every wood-train. Red Cloud drilled his warriors daily, seeming to possess a system of signals equally as good as those in use at the fort. Colonel Carrington, in his description of the events at the post, said on one occasion that Red Cloud's signals covered a line of seven miles, and were rapidly and accurately displayed.

On 6 December 1866, a number of soldiers were killed, and on the 21st, the picket signaled that the wagon train was surrounded, and 99 men were sent to its relief. Afterward, it was ascertained that the train was threatened but not attacked. In fact, the teams and escort came in safely that night.

Red Cloud had created a brilliant feint to draw troops some distance from the post so he could engage them successfully. The entire command under Fetterman and Brown was killed.

Red Cloud's defeat of Fetterman propelled him into an unprecedented role of leadership among the Sioux. He became supreme chief. Hundreds of recruits joined his camp. He was given an immense 'medicine dance' and heralded as invincible.

On 2 August 1867, Major James Powell was attacked by a large force under the command of Red Cloud and Spotted Tail. In this fight, Red Cloud and his warriors exhibited, with scarcely an exception, the greatest bravery ever shown by Native Americans in the history of the West.

Unknown to the Native Americans, special wagon-beds, constructed of iron, were mounted on wheels by the Army blacksmiths. When the attack began, the troops removed these from the trucks and placed them in a small circle and concealed themselves beneath. The iron was sufficiently heavy to stop or deflect bullets, and the men were armed with the Winchester repeating rifles not previously used by the army on the Plains. The Native Americans could not understand how so small a body of men could fire with such rapidity.

Red Cloud said to Spotted Tail, as the two sat their horses on a little knoll a few hundred yards distant, that he believed the Americans had 'medicine guns,' which never ceased firing. The entire force of the Sioux and Cheyenne was hurled against the enemy, Red Cloud's nephew distinguishing himself by riding among the foremost and the two chiefs accompanying the charge.

Red Cloud charged no less than eight or ten times, frequently coming within 30 or 40 feet. Many of his dead fell less than 20 yards from the improvised fortification. One Indian fell near enough to touch the beds with his coup-stick before he died. Nearly half of Red Cloud's magnificent force of warriors had made their last assault.

'I lost them,' he said when, as an old man and at peace, he talked of the days of war. 'They never fought again.'

Red Cloud agreed at last to meet with a Peace Commission. For a month, beginning on 13 August 1867, he attended a council in which Red Cloud was promised that the settlers would evacuate and not trespass in large areas of Sioux hunting grounds.

In October 1867, the southern peoples gathered at Medicine Lodge Creek to meet in council with representatives of the 'Great White Father.' The Kiowa, Comanche, Arapaho and Cheyenne agreed, after much discussion, that they would settle south of the Arkansas River.

ABOVE: CHIEF SPOTTED TAIL SPEAKING AT THE 1868 TREATY SIGNING THAT CONCLUDED THE 'RED CLOUD WAR.' *OPPOSITE:* CHIEF QUANAH PARKER OF THE COMANCHE WAS, LIKE RED CLOUD, A HIGHLY REGARDED LEADER.

At the same time the Sioux and the peoples of the north were expected to assemble at Fort Laramie. The Peace Commission had planned a treaty with the Sioux to follow the one in the South, but Red Cloud did not wish to negotiate until all the forts were removed from the Montana country. As it was impractical to remove forts at the beginning of the winter, the commissioners asked Red Cloud for a truce until spring. When spring came the forts were abandoned.

Red Cloud came to meet the Peace Commission in April 1868. Both Red Cloud and Chief Spotted Tail spoke, and the commissioners promised that settlers would be kept out of the Sioux country and that the Sioux would be supplied with food, clothing, plows, cattle and schools. 'From this day forward,' read the treaty, 'all war among the parties to this agreement shall forever cease.'

The conflict that had come to be known as 'Red Cloud's War' was over. After this council, Red Cloud retired from warfare, and became a Native American senior statesman. Younger men, such as Spotted Tail and Sitting Bull, would take up the fight that would come to a bitter, brutal climax within a decade.

Red Cloud was friendly with Sitting Bull, but was seldom associated with him either in councils or upon the field. The two present marked contrasts. The latter was very outspoken in his hatred of the whites, but lacked the tact and judgment displayed by Red Cloud in his later years. Sitting Bull's temper was easily ruffled, and even as late as 1890 (he was killed on 15 December 1890) he persisted in open censure of government authorities.

When Red Cloud settled on a reservation near Fort Robinson, Sitting Bull continued to ride the traditional hunting grounds in the mountains and in the valleys of the Tongue, Powder, Yellowstone and Big Horn rivers of Montana Territory. Some of the turbulent element in Red Cloud's camp joined him, but by far the greater portion of those who followed Sitting Bull were not Oglalas.

Despite the dishonesty of many of the American agents at the reservation, Red Cloud remained faithful to his treaty promises.

In spite of suffering, privation and thefts of every description, Red Cloud and his people kept their faith.

'How can you expect us to take the white man's road when you move us before we have time to plant and grow corn?' he complained. 'To clear the ground and raise cattle?'

In 1874, he was part of a delegation of Native Americans that went to Washington, where they were flattered and promised many things. Meanwhile, it had been decided by the Commissioner of Indian Affairs to remove the Sioux to the Missouri River, where some good soil assured corn and wheat. Red Cloud and Spotted Tail begged that they be not sent there, for whisky was brought up the river and sold to their young men.

In May, the Commissioner of Indian Affairs himself went to meet with them. When he rose to speak, Chief Spotted Tail jumped to his feet and walked toward him, waving in his hand the paper containing the promise of the government to return them to White Clay Creek.

'All the men who come from Washington are liars,' he began, 'and the bald-headed ones are the worst of all! I don't want to hear one word from you — you are a bald-headed old liar! You have but one thing to do here, and that is to give an order for us to return to White Clay Creek. Here are your written words, and if you don't give this order, and everything here is not on wheels inside of ten days, I'll order my young men to tear down and burn everything in this part of the country! I don't want to hear anything more from you, and I've got nothing more to say to you.'

He turned his back on the Commissioner and walked away. Such language would not have been accepted from unarmed and helpless Native Americans, but when it came from a chief with 4000 armed warriors at his back, it was another affair altogether.

The order was written. In less than ten days everything was 'on wheels' and the whole body of the Sioux on the move to the country they had indicated, and the Secretary of the Interior wrote, naively, in his report: 'The Indians were found to be quite determined to move westward, and the promise of the government in that respect was faithfully kept.'

In 1875, gold was discovered in the Black Hills, and settlers and miners flocked into the new territory, trespassing on the land granted to the Sioux. They promptly retaliated, and the US Government sent the flamboyant Colonel (formerly with the temporary rank of general) George Armstrong Custer to remove the miners from the new gold fields.

He successfully scattered the invaders, without a shot being fired at Native Americans.

For his part, Red Cloud had kept his treaty promise, but peace was not long to be maintained. The frontier towns began to fill up with outcasts of civilization and the 'breeders of mischief.' No sooner had Custer returned from his expedition than the miners flocked back to the gulches around Deadwood in what is now South Dakota.

Meanwhile, the buffalo-hunters were fast destroying the great herds, and Red Cloud beheld this with a heavy heart. The death-knell of his people's freedom and prosperity on the Plains was sounded in the noise of the train, the blast in the mine, and the din in the town.

He could not go to war himself because he imagined a responsibility to his people on the reservations, but he sent many of his best warriors to join Crazy Horse, American Horse and the other radicals. Open warfare escalated, and in June 1876, Custer was ordered to the Little Big Horn to destroy the villages of the Sioux and Cheyenne.

The battle, the largest in the history of warfare on the Plains, was a resounding victory for the Native Americans, but the die was cast. The battle proved that the two sides could not successfully co-exist without the Native Americans being confined to reservations, and the US Army ultimately had the power to impose its will upon the Native Americans.

Many Sioux surrendered after the summer of 1876 and were returned to their respective agencies. Sitting Bull and his most faithful followers fled to Canada, where he remained for some time. General MacKenzie took nearly all of Red Cloud's horses shortly after the Battle of the Little Big Horn in order to prevent further hostilities.

On 3 September 1877, a soldier ran a bayonet into Crazy Horse while the latter was confined as a prisoner of war in the guardhouse of Fort Robinson. The murder led to talk of war among the Sioux, but Red Cloud intervened and counseled peace. The alternative would have been a disaster.

Red Cloud and his people were moved again, this time to the Ridge Agency. He appealed to Washington for reimbursement for the ponies stolen by lawless men, and for an improvement in the condition of his people. A Congressional Committee visited Pine Ridge in 1883 and found Red Cloud and 8000 people living in deplorable conditions.

After the Wounded Knee massacre of December 1890, many Sioux left the reservations and fled north. Red Cloud, with his daughter and son, in spite of his protests, were compelled to accompany them. Jack Red Cloud, his son, smuggled him out of camp, and his daughter led him 18 miles through a severe blizzard, back to Pine Ridge.

Nearly blind, Red Cloud aged rapidly after 1890, but during the last years of his life Red Cloud enjoyed the comforts of a two-story frame house given to him by the government.

To his visitors, he spoke of the happy 'buffalo days,' and the free life of the Plains.

'You see this barren waste?' He once asked. 'We have a little land along the creek which affords good grazing, but we must use some of it for corn and wheat. There are other creeks which have bottoms like this, but most of the land is poor and worthless. Think of it! I, who used to own rich soil in a well-watered country so extensive that I could not ride through it in a week on my fastest pony, am put down here! Why, I have to go five miles for wood for my fire. Washington took our lands and promised to feed and support us. Now I, who used to control 5000 warriors, must tell Washington when I am hungry. I must beg for that which I own. If I beg hard, they put me in the guardhouse. We have trouble. Our girls are getting bad. Coughing sickness every winter carries away our best people. My heart is heavy, I am old, I cannot do much more. Young man, I wish there was someone to help my poor people when I am gone.'

Throughout a stormy period in American history, Red Cloud figured as a brave warrior, a dignified counselor, and a staunch advocate of the welfare of his people. His bearing was such as one might expect in a man who has faced death upon the field of battle, but after the treaty of 1868, he and his immediate followers observed their part of the agreement, although the white people gave them every pretext for violation.

Red Cloud possessed a great human kindness. In his 20 years at Pine Ridge, he exhibited a quiet and gentle demeanor. He lamented the fate of his people, but there was no bitterness.

ABOVE: BLACK DOG OF THE SANTEE SIOUX WAS ONE OF THE GENERATION OF LEADERS WHO PRECEDED RED CLOUD. *OPPOSITE:* THE SAME IS TRUE OF STEEP WIND OF THE SANS ARC SIOUX. BOTH PORTRAITS ARE BY GEORGE CATLIN.

SATANK and SATANTA

At the signing of the milestone Treaty of Medicine Lodge Creek in 1867, the name which was first on the list of Kiowa chiefs was that of Setangya, known to the Europeans as Satank, or Sitting Bear. Next in order was that of Satanta, or White Bear, his second in command, a warrior two decades younger than Satank.

Satank had long been a chief of the Kiowa. He was among the young warriors when the Kiowa and Comanche made peace with the Cheyenne and Arapaho on the banks of the Arkansas in 1840, following the advice of William Bent. Even then he was a recognized leader and a maker of potent medicine.

Six years later, in 1873, he was the head of a delegation taken to visit President James Knox Polk in Washington. 'A fine looking man of good size and middle age, and evidently a man of talents,' the President found him.

Satank's own comment on this visit to the United States capital was that the European-Americans were more numerous than the stars and he gave up trying to count them.

After signing the Treaty of Medicine Lodge Creek, the Kiowa and Comanche remained in a state of strained relations with the Texans because the new reservation was close to the Texas border. In response to an incident that occurred in September 1871, Satank, Satanta, and Big Tree were taken by US Army soldiers, but Satank was not to go to Texas for trial. Instead, the three chiefs were to be taken to Fort Sill, Oklahoma.

When the party was about a mile from Fort Sill, Satank sang his death chant and tore the fetters from his wrists. He sprang on his guard with a knife which he had hidden beneath his shirt. A shot ended his rebellion and his life.

Satanta and Big Tree were turned over to the Texas authorities and stood trial. The verdict was murder, and the sentence, death by hanging. Milder counsels prevailed and the sentence was commuted to life imprisonment.

They spent two years in the Texas State Penitentiary, and in their absence, Lone Wolf was chief and spokesman for the Kiowa. He refused to cooperate with the army until Satanta and Big Tree were released. A council called by a coalition of Native American groups from Indian Territory had no effect upon the determination of the Kiowa. The United States Government appealed to the Governor of Texas to exercise clemency, and the two chiefs were released on parole.

In June 1874 the general bad feelings held toward the Kiowa resulted in open warfare. The opening battle would, alas, be the Kiowa/Comanche Waterloo. In the Texas panhandle stood the old adobe walls that had long been a landmark for Native Americans and Europeans, the remains of the southern fort of the Bent brothers, long abandoned and left to the slow

erosion of sun and wind. Here, in 1864, Kit Carson had fought his last and fiercest battle. Now, ten years later, a group of European-American buffalo hunters were using it as a headquarters and rendezvous point.

Isatai, a Comanche shaman, had promised them that he would protect them against all harm and assure their complete victory. The Kiowa made the attack on Sunday morning, when the hunters were in camp. A weekday would have been a far wiser choice.

The Battle of Adobe Walls, as it came to known, was a setback for the Kiowa and Comanche, and by September 1874, Colonel Ranald Mackenzie's troopers had compelled Satanta to surrender. Lone Wolf remained free until February 1875, when he rode into Fort Sill to give himself up. Having served time in federal custody in Florida, he died of malaria in 1879.

Satanta, transferred in irons to Huntsville, Alabama, was thrown into a federal prison. In 1878, he was killed while in custody when he fell from a second story window. The official verdict was suicide.

ABOVE: THE GREAT KIOWA LEADER SATANK, OR SITTING BEAR, PHOTOGRAPHED BY WILLIAM SOULE IN 1870. *OPPOSITE:* SATANTA, OR WHITE BEAR, ALSO PHOTOGRAPHED BY SOULE IN 1870.

CAPTAIN JACK

Until the 1850s, European settlement in what is now California was restricted largely to Russian hunting outposts and the areas around the series of missions that the Spanish had built in the coastal valleys between San Diego and the San Francisco Bay Area. Impact upon the Native peoples of the region had been minimal except in the regions of Southern California, where the Native Americans interacted with the Spanish.

The Gold Rush of 1848 and 1849 had changed that, bringing tens and soon hundreds of thousands of people into California. In 1850, California became a state of the United States. Both San Francisco and Sacramento became overnight metropolises.

Among the great Native peoples of North America, history is filled with many mentions of the Iroquois, the Sioux and the Cheyenne. So many peoples of lesser population have been relegated to the status of footnotes. The Modoc were such a people, too small a people — only a few hundred at most — to attract much notice. Indeed, their home was among the lava beds area of northeastern California, a thousand miles from San Diego, as far as the distance from New York to Chicago.

However, for a few months in 1872 and 1873, the country waited breathlessly for the news of their activities and those of their remarkable and mercurial leader. This man's name was Kientpoos, or Kintpuash, though he took the English name Captain Jack. He gained his name by his fondness for an army officer's uniform jacket that was part of his usual attire.

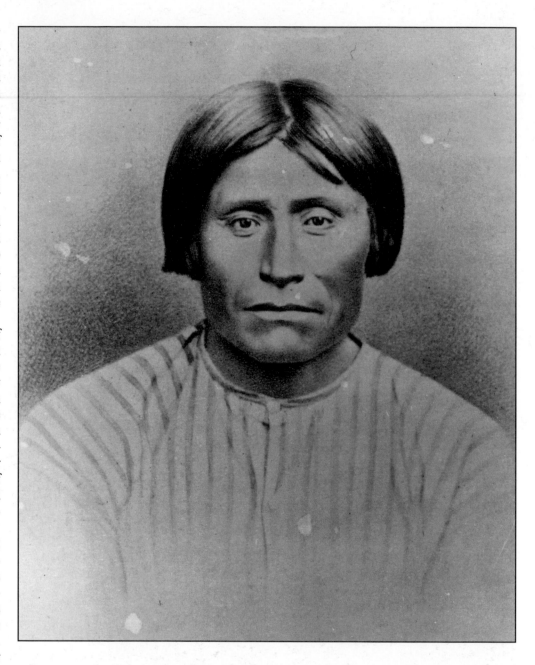

The Modoc, in a loosely united band, hunted in the Tule Lake country, where Oregon and California meet. South of the lake was a lava-covered area, traversed by jagged rock gullies and sown with black stones whose edges cut the feet of man or horse.

Not far from here were the Klamath, ancient enemies of the Modoc. Under the ill-conceived policy of placing Native peoples on reservations, the government assigned to the Modoc a place on the Klamath reservation. There was room enough so far as land was concerned, but there is never room for enemies to live together. The Klamath were the stronger,

and the little Modoc band was harried from one point to another. Finally they pulled up stakes and returned to their old home on Lost River near the lava beds.

Following in the footsteps of great men like Tecumseh, Captain Jack was a strong believer in the idea that the Modoc should live forever in Northern California, and objected strongly whenever a proposition was broached of a return to the Klamath land.

He and those who agreed to his notion asked instead that they be given a place to stay on Lost River. However, the situation of Captain Jack, with his handful of followers was not analogous to Red Cloud, who had been backed by the guns of thousands. The Indian Office refused his request, asking that

troops be sent to round up the band and return it to the reservation.

In the autumn of 1872, the Modoc resisted arrest and retreated to their stronghold — the lava beds. Here, in the rocks they knew well, they were able to remain perfectly concealed.

At first the US Army soldiers laughed at the boast of Captain Jack that he could hold off a thousand soldiers. But after a few days of fighting in the 'land of burnt-out fires,' of receiving the bullets of an unseen enemy as they struggled over the jagged rocks, there was no more laughter.

Captain Jack had not boasted. He had spoken simple truth.

Negotiations followed, and the US Army sent General E S Canby, an earnest advocate of peace and a good friend of the Native American, as well as a soldier of experience and reputation.

Throughout the winter, and into early 1873, messages came and went between Captain Jack and his band in the lava beds, and the Peace Commission headed by General Canby. Captain Jack continued to demand a reservation on Lost River and immunity for alleged 'crimes' committed by the Modocs.

As spring came, an agreement seemed as far off as ever.

A conference had been postponed by the army, but a second conference was proposed by the Modoc, and the commission accepted, though there were indications of general mistrust.

Winema, a Modoc woman also known as Toby Riddle, whose European husband was the interpreter for the commission, knew that there was danger even though the commissioners had given the Native Americans their promise to come unarmed.

General Canby and Dr Eleazar Thomas, the remaining two commissioners, declared that their honor was pledged to carry out the council as agreed upon. Both were well known to be

ABOVE: SCAR-FACED CHARLIE, ONE OF THE MODOC VETERANS OF THE 1873 LAVA BEDS CAMPAIGN. *OPPOSITE:* A GRIM-FACED CAPTAIN JACK. *ABOVE LEFT:* TOBY RIDDLE'S NATIVE NAME WAS WINEMA, WHICH MEANS WOMAN OF THE BRAVE HEART. SHE WAS CAPTAIN JACK'S COUSIN.

the Modoc's sincerest friends. According to witnesses, it seemed apparent that these Native Americans were armed. There was a brief and excited discussion in which Captain Jack's demands were firm. According to the official story of events, Captain Jack took out a gun and shot General Canby in the face. Jack's colleague, Boston Charlie, is said to have then killed Dr Thomas.

The Modoc band fled back to the shelter of their caves in the lava beds after this confused melee, but after several weeks of desperate fighting, they were captured. Captain Jack and three others met death on the scaffold about a year after the beginning of the outbreak of the conflict.

The others who survived were sent en masse to Baxter Springs, Kansas and quietly located at Quapaw Agency in the northeastern corner of the Indian Territory.

SITTING BULL

He stands tall among the most prominent of all Native American leaders, a stern and dramatic figure praised by some and feared by others. He typified the Plains spirit of the nineteenth century. He bluntly told white people that they lied. He refused to accept substitutes for solemn treaties. He lived and died a strong, resourceful man. He presents one of the most picturesque characters among the Native Americans in any period of American history.

He lived as a warrior and shaman, yet he travelled to Europe as part of William Cody's Wild West Show. Against this backdrop, he was out of place in the reservation life of 1880-1890.

'God Almighty made me,' he told General Nelson Miles on the occasion of their first meeting. 'God Almighty did not make me an agency Indian, and I'll fight and die fighting before any white man can make me an agency Indian.'

His prophecy was fulfilled.

Born in 1834, he was called Jumping Badger as a boy, and at the age of 14 he accompanied his father into batttle, in which he counted his first coup against an enemy. In 1848, his name became Tatanka Yotaka (Tatankya Iyotake), which literally means 'sitting buffalo bull,' although he was generally known simply as Sitting Bull. He was of the Hunkpapa (Uncpapa) division of the Sioux tribe. His boyhood, as with that of Red Cloud and other prominent Native Americans, was spent among his own people in the hunt for buffalo, at the village, and occasionally he accompanied war parties. His name (after boyhood) was Four Horn, but when he became a shaman in 1857, his name was changed to Sitting Bull.

He rapidly acquired influence in his own band, being especially skillful in the character of peacemaker. He took an active part in the Plains wars of the 1860s, and first became widely known to the European-Americans in 1866, when he led a memorable raid against Fort Buford. Sitting Bull was active in his opposition to white settlement almost continuously from 1869 to 1876. During this time, he also came into conflict with the Crow and the Shoshone.

By this time, Red Cloud had made peace, but other Sioux had not. These included the Oglala division, led by Crazy Horse, as well as those led by Sitting Bull and Gall of the Hunkpapa, and by Two Moons of the Northern Cheyenne.

The treaty of 1868 had submitted to Red Cloud's condition that the forts along the Bozeman Trail be abandoned and the road leading to them closed. The noted generals who framed that treaty perhaps thought that although they could not control the Native American, they might be able to control the European-American. Six years later it was obvious they could do neither. The march of European settlement was going up the Bozeman Trail just as surely as it had gone down the Ohio and up the Missouri.

The Army itself could not enforce the treaty. The word had circulated that gold had been discovered in the Black Hills area of Dakota Territory, an area guaranteed to the Sioux under the treaty. If it had been difficult before to keep the European-Americans away, it was impossible now.

In 1874, Colonel (formerly temporary Brigadier General) George Armstrong Custer of the 7th Cavalry led an exploratory expedition to the Black Hills area of Dakota Territory. The stated purpose was to evict non-Native people. The Indian Bureau had no realization of the number of Sioux present. The Pawnee knew more about the matter, for when the bands had fewer Europeans to disturb them they were able to pay more attention to their Native American foes. The Pawnee agent reported it as a good year that had seen only a half-dozen Sioux raids, and not more than a score or two of his people had fallen victim to their ancient enemies.

The reverse of the coin was that the Sioux had to stay in the Black Hills. Sitting Bull, Gall and Crazy Horse believed that they could go wherever they wished, including their traditional hunting grounds on the watershed of the Yellowstone River in southeastern Montana Territory.

The order was issued that these recalcitrant Native American men, known as Sitting Bull's Band on the Yellowstone, must come in to the agency and be enrolled with the Native Americans who were receiving their supplies from the government. Forty thousand of the Sioux were being rationed at this time, a pound of beef and a pound of flour daily for each of them.

The beginning of 1876 was set as the deadline. The year began, and the Sioux did not come in to enroll. In February, the army took the matter in hand. Sitting Bull, meanwhile, had issued his call. Emissaries went to all the 12 Sioux agencies and to peoples far and near, eastward even to the Chippewa, and westward far beyond the Rockies. While most of the peoples declined, a considerable number of the Sioux of all the bands found their way to his camp.

In his report for 1875, the Commissioner of Indian Affairs said quite confidently that the Sioux in Montana 'could not muster more than 300 warriors.' A year later he had a very different opinion.

US Army Chief of Staff and Civil War hero General Philip Sheridan designed a grand three-pronged offensive set for June 1876, and aimed at the defeat of the Sioux. Colonel John Gibbon was marching from the western part of Montana. General George Crook was coming up from Wyoming to the south. General Alfred Terry, whose force included Colonel Custer's 7th Cavalry, started out to the westward from Fort Abraham Lincoln on the Missouri River.

Each commander hoped he would be the one to meet the enemy and win a decisive victory. Crook's engagement on the Rosebud River with the warriors of Crazy Horse on 17 June was far from a victory. When the Sioux withdrew at the end of two hours' severe fighting, Crook realized that he could not

CHIEF SITTING BULL
SIOUX -

pursue. He must return for supplies and to care for his wounded. The Sioux and their Cheyenne allies had given the troops a decided check.

Custer did not know of this engagement when he rode out from the camp on the Powder River a few days later. His orders were to meet Gibbon on 26 June near the Little Big Horn. He was there a day earlier and met, instead, the great encampment of Native Americans.

Custer's scouts were Crow and Arikara, and his guide, Mitch Buoyer, was half French and half Sioux. Buoyer warned Custer that the Native American village they were approaching was of immense proportions. Opinions differ as to the number

of Native Americans camped in this site on the shores of the Little Big Horn River. It was a great village stretching down the valley almost as far as the eye could reach. Sitting Bull, Gall and Crazy Horse were there, along with all of their followers, the families of their followers, and a large number of Cheyenne. While an investigator said there could have been no more than 1200 warriors with their women and children in Sitting Bull's camp, contemporary and later estimates by soldiers and Native American scouts ranged from 2000 to 6000 warriors, and as many as 25,000 people total.

Custer's vastly inferior force of 600 was divided into three detachments, each isolated from the others during the engagement. Major Marcus Reno and his men, attacking one end of the great Sioux camp, were repulsed and bottled up on a hill. They knew nothing of what was going on elsewhere. Captain Frederick Benteen, with the pack trains, came up too late to take any part or be of any assistance. Custer himself, with 215 men, rode along the ridge above the river to the attack. Both Crazy Horse and Gall led their forces to attack him, and in half an hour, not one of the soldiers was left alive.

After the battle, Sitting Bull is said to have remarked gloomily, 'Now the soldiers will give us no rest.'

The Native Americans separated into two parties, one, under Crazy Horse, being defeated in December, and the other, under Sitting Bull, continuing toward Canada to escape capture. Crazy Horse himself would be dead within the year.

By the spring of 1877 a number of the Sioux returned to the United States, but it was five years before Sitting Bull left Canada. Sitting Bull is said to have proclaimed that he was an English subject, that his people had accepted English rule after the French and Indian War and had never recognized the authority of the United States. He shook hands with Her Majesty's representatives in Canada and declined to return to the United States until 1881.

In that year, he surrendered at Fort Buford under a promise of amnesty and was sent to Fort Randall until 1883.

TOP: A LITHOGRAPH OF SITTING BULL WHICH APPEARED AFTER HIS DEATH. BELOW: COLONEL CUSTER AND HIS TROOPERS AT THE BATTLE OF THE LITTLE BIGHORN. OPPOSITE: GALL WAS ONE OF SITTING BULL'S KEY COLLEAGUES, AND AN IMPORTANT SIOUX LEADER AT THE LITTLE BIGHORN.

In 1883 a Congressional Commission, composed of H L Dawes, John A Logan, Angus Cameron, John T Morgan and George G Vest, visited Standing Rock Agency to investigate conditions. There had been great discontent because of the failure of the government to fulfill the stipulations set forth in the treaty of 1868. Sitting Bull was eloquent and steadfast in speaking out for the rights of the Native people under the treaty, insistent that the cattle and goods promised them be forthcoming and was rather against the further division of the reservation.

Although he had surrendered and gone upon a reservation, Sitting Bull continued unreconciled. It was through his influence that the Sioux refused to sell their lands in 1888, and it was at his camp at Standing Rock Agency, and at his invitation, that Kicking Bear organized the Ghost Dance on the reservation in 1890. In the meantime, he enjoyed a great deal of notoriety throughout the eastern United States and in Europe as a member of William 'Buffalo Bill' Cody's Wild West Show. He was lionized and his photographs and autographs were extremely popular. What a strange contrast it must have been between the glittering palaces of Europe and the harsh reality of the life at Standing Rock reservation to which he returned!

In 1890, he broke his peace pipe — deliberately. All his followers saw him. He had kept it since his return from Canada in 1881. But now it was destroyed. This was equivalent to saying to Washington, 'I break with you.'

Word of Sitting Bull's action was carried to the Standing Rock Indian agent, Major James McLaughlin, who decided to take the chief into custody. At dawn on 15 December 1890, 40 Indian Police officers under Lieutenant Bull Head arrested Sitting Bull. One of Sitting Bull's followers and an old enemy of Bull Head, shot the lieutenant, who squeezed off a shot as he fell, mortally wounded. This last shot killed Sitting Bull. The words of his prediction were verified — he never became a reservation Indian.

Sitting Bull was never an agency Indian. He lived in the past. He was tolerant of the white man and his ways because he was compelled to co-exist with the white man. Sitting Bull's

own son, Crow Foot, believed in his father's 'medicine' and died with him. Truly, there is no greater proof of faith.

Sitting Bull had been the incarnation of the fighting spirit of the Sioux. A man possessed of the ability of Sitting Bull, in a different environment, would have become a leader of great nations. Like his Prussian contemporary, Otto Eduard Leopold von Bismarck, whom he may have met in Europe, Sitting Bull was a man of blood and iron, who led his followers into action, although the cause for which he fought was virtually hopeless.

As Major McLaughlin wrote, 'His accuracy of judgment, knowledge of men, a student-like disposition to observe natural phenomena, and a deep insight into affairs among Indians and such white people as he came into contact with, made his stock in trade, and made "good medicine." He stood well among his own people and was respected for his generosity, quiet disposition, and steadfast adherence to Indian ideals.'

Sitting Bull. Squaw and Teepe.

Sitting Bull's address to the Government Peace Commission (1883)

I am here by the will of the Great Spirit, and by His will I am a chief. My heart is sweet, and I know it is sweet, because whatever passes near me puts out its tongue to me, and yet you men have come here to talk with us, and you say you do not know who I am. I want to tell you that if the Great Spirit has chosen anyone to be the chief of this country it is myself.

I came in with a glad heart to shake hands with you, my friends, for I feel that I have displeased you, and I am here to apologize to you for my bad conduct and to take back what I said. I will take it back because I consider I have made your hearts bad. I heard that you were coming here from the Great Father's house some time before you came, and I have been sitting here like a prisoner waiting for someone to release me. I was looking for you everywhere, and I considered that when we talked with you it was the same as if we were talking with the Great Father, and I believe that what I pour out from my heart the Great Father will hear. What I take back is what I said to cause the people to leave the council, and want to apologize for leaving myself. The people acted like children, and I am sorry for it. I was very sorry when I found out that your intentions were good and entirely different from what I supposed they were.

Now I will tell you my mind and I will tell everything straight. I know the Great Spirit is looking down upon me from

above and will hear what I say. Therefore I will do my best to talk straight, and I hope that someone will listen to my wishes and help me to carry them out.

I have always been a chief, and have been made chief of all the land. Thirty-two years ago I was present at councils with the white man, and at the time of the Fort Rice council I was on the prairie listening to it, and since then a great many questions have been asked about it. When the Black Hills council was held, and they asked me to give up that land, I said they must wait.

When we sold the Black Hills we got a very small price for it, and not what we ought to have received. I used to think that the size of the payments would remain the same all the time,

ABOVE LEFT: SITTING BULL AND HIS WIFE, TRAVORIET, AT FORT RANDALL, DAKOTA TERRITORY, IN 1882. *ABOVE:* SITTING BULL WITH HIS FAMILY AT THEIR LOG HOUSE ON THE PINE RIDGE RESERVATION, CIRCA 1890.

but they are growing smaller all the time. I want you to tell the Great Father everything I have said, and that we want some benefit from the promises he has made us, and I don't think I should be tormented with anything about giving up any part of my land until those promises are fulfilled. I would rather wait until that time, when I will be ready to transact any business he may desire.

I consider that my country takes in the Black Hills, and runs from the Powder River to the Missouri, and that all of this land belongs to me. Our reservation is not as large as we want it to be, and I suppose the Great Father owes us money now for land he has taken from us in the past. You white men advise us to follow your ways, and therefore I talk as I do. When you

have a piece of land, and anything trespasses on it, you catch it and keep it until you get damages, and I am doing the same thing now, and I want you to tell all this to the Great Father for me.

I am looking into the future for the benefit of my children, and that is what I mean when I say I want my country taken care of for me. My children will grow up here, and I am looking ahead for their benefit, and for the benefit of my children's children, too, and even beyond that again.

JOSEPH

By the winter of 1885, the Native Americans living on the Plains in the United States and Canada were faced with a crisis as the once vast herds of buffalo upon which they depended had been hunted nearly to exhaustion. Meanwhile, across the northern Rockies to the west, the Native peoples, while culturally similar in many ways to the Plains people, did not depend on the buffalo.

To the west and north, for the Native Americans of the Pacific Northwest, the principal 'subsistence type,' or source of protein, was the Pacific salmon. The same was true of the peoples of the mountains west of the northern Rockies — notably the Nez Perce — who fished the rivers and streams into which the Pacific salmon came to spawn. While the salmon 'runs' are seasonal, the precise hour for the salmon to appear varies. Three varieties of salmon ran in the streams accessible to the Nez Perce people, and since they did not run at the same time, there were several periods during the year when a lot of fish could be had for the taking. At such times the surplus fish were dried, smoked and stored for the future.

Horses probably reached the Nez Perce early in eighteenth century, and they had about the same effect as in the case of buffalo hunting Plains peoples. Horses gave them a mobility that had never before been possible. It is interesting that in the valleys above the Columbia River, the methods of using the horse were the same as in the Plains, and that along with this went a similarity in dress, house furnishings and the use of the tepee.

Few Europeans entered this country before 1800. In 1840, Marcus Whitman set up a mission near Walla Walla (now in Washington state), but seven years later the Cayuse Indians burned the mission. In the years after the Civil War, however, settlers began staking out claims near the headwaters of the Columbia, in the valleys west of the northern Rockies. Soon they were in conflict with the powerful Nez Perce.

The most highly regarded of Nez Perce leaders, and indeed one of the most important of Native American orators ever, was Hinmaton Yalatkit, a man known to European people as Chief Joseph. Indeed, he may be said to have rescued this people from oblivion by skilled leadership in a war, albeit ultimately unsuccessful, with the United States. He won the first skirmish, but from then until the end was in full retreat. The retreat is what intrigues us, the wonder being that he had military genius enough to escape annihilation.

By 1877, he was a recognized leader, probably 35 years old. He had some knowledge of English and the ways of European

ABOVE: HINMATON YALATKIT, KNOWN AS JOSEPH. *OPPOSITE:* A GROUP OF NEZ PERCE HORSEMEN, PHOTOGRAPHED BY MAJOR LEE MOORHOUSE IN JULY 1906, TWO YEARS AFTER JOSEPH DIED.

people. In 1863 his people had entered into a treaty by which they agreed to give up roaming about and settle on a reservation near Fort Lapwai.

When it came to a final decision, they were reluctant to move, and temporized until about 1877, when the Indian agent ordered them to comply. A part of the people did so, but Joseph's people refused. Joseph himself recommended compliance, but his followers favored resistance. Joseph knew that now war was inevitable, that his people had begun it, and he was not reluctant to assume the leadership. He and his people were confident that they could defeat all the troops sent against them.

Joseph took up a defensive position in White Bird Canyon near the Salmon River in Idaho. On 16 June 1877, a small detachment of United States troops attacked, but were forced to retreat with relatively heavy losses. Joseph had won the opening round, and the Nez Perce left their strong position, retiring to the Clear Water River near Kamia, Idaho.

Soon, a larger body of troops under General Oliver O Howard came upon him. Joseph had to give battle, but this time he was outfought. His only chance lay in keeping ahead of the pursuing troops, turning upon advance and scouting parties when he had a chance to overwhelm them. He was well equipped with horses, well armed, and well supplied with ammunition. However, his whole band was with him — women, children, the aged, the sick and the wounded. His advantage lay in knowing the country, and in how to live off the land.

Joseph headed toward Montana by way of Yellowstone National Park. There were several skirmishes between Joseph's rear guard and outriders from Howard's troops, but nothing decisive, except that every loss to the Native Americans was Howard's gain.

At Canyon Creek, just west of Billings, Montana, Colonel Samuel Sturgis, in command of the 7th Cavalry, caught up with Joseph, but he escaped. Joseph planned to reach the Musselshell River and, if still pursued, to continue north into Canada. Meanwhile, Howard had with him a body of Native American scouts who, in one way and another, got information as to Joseph's plans.

Near what is now Miles City, Montana, was a body of troops under General Nelson 'Bearcoat' Miles. He was ordered to intercept the Nez Perce. So when Joseph and his weary followers reached a point — only 40 miles from Canada — near the Bear Paw Mountains, south of the town of Chinook on the Milk River, he found a new army blocking his way. General Howard was close upon his heels, so at last Joseph found himself in a trap. In fact General Miles surprised him, rushed his camp and captured most of his horses. Yet the Native Americans dug rifle pits and prepared to fight.

Neither Howard nor Miles wished to exterminate his band, so they gave Joseph time to consider a surrender. His final speech, delivered on 5 October 1877, ranks with one of the greatest ever delivered by any military leader in defeat:

'I am tired of fighting. Our chiefs are killed. Looking Glass is dead. Toohulhulsote is dead. The old men are all dead. It is the young men who say yes or no. He who led the young men is dead. It is cold and we have no blankets. The little children are freezing to death. My people, some of them, have run away to the hills and have no blankets, no food. No one knows where they are — perhaps freezing to death. I want to have time to look for my children and see how many of them I can find. Maybe I shall find them among the dead. Hear me, my chiefs. I am tired. My heart is sick and sad. From where the sun now stands I will fight no more forever.'

Joseph had made a masterly retreat of over a thousand miles. Yet he was doomed from the start. Had he reached Canada, his fate would not have been improved. After surrendering, he was not permitted to return to the reservation he refused in 1877, but some of his party were returned. Joseph was carried to Oklahoma as a prisoner of war, and many years later, he and his most faithful followers were sent to the Colville Reservation, in Washington state, where he died on 21 September 1904.

GERONIMO

The Apache were nomadic warriors who lived in the mountains and deserts throughout northern Mexico and the southwestern territories of the United States. Linguistically the Apache are related to the Navaho, and like them, call themselves *Tinneh,* meaning 'the people.'

The Apache were the last of North America's native people to surrender to the will of the US Government. This was partly because of their will to survive in freedom and in part because their native lands were considered inhospitable by most of the European-Americans until late in the nineteenth century. The Apache adapted well to the hot, dry Southwest. They could traverse a country and gather sustenance where the European would perish. They could find shelter in a land so bare that a cactus plant is a tree and a depression in the sand a river bed.

The Apache feuded with the Pueblo Indians, resisted the Spanish and fought the Mexican people for centuries. When American settlers came into Arizona, these newcomers were not welcomed.

The great Mimbreno Apache chief, Mangas Coloradas, was the most eminent of senior Apache statesmen, and the one who set the tone for relations with settlers for the latter half of the nineteenth century. He had been one of those who met with General Philip Kearny when he surveyed the region for the United States in 1846. His alliance with Cochise of the Chiricahua division of the Apache made him an important leader in the Southwest, and one with whom the US Government felt it should deal. In the meantime, both chiefs were strongly in disfavor of European settlements.

Mangas Coloradas was ambushed by American soldiers, captured and murdered in January 1863, leaving the 51-year-old Cochise as the Apache's most celebrated leader.

The relations between the settlers and the Apache, which had always been strained, deteriorated into a virtual state of war by the end of the 1860s. This led President (formerly General) Ulysses S Grant to take action. He asked General Oliver O Howard to lead a force into Arizona to stabilize the situation. The measure of his undertaking may be gauged from one of his initial difficulties, which was persuading the citizens of Arizona to return to the Native Americans a group of captured children they were holding as servants or hostages.

General Howard was inclined to feel that the children should go back to their relatives, the Arivaipa Apache, but the governor and attorney general of the territory protested strongly, threatening to appeal to the attorney general of the United States. Against their protest, the soldier-commissioner decided to put the young captives in escrow with a kindly sergeant's wife, pending the decision of the president. The decision was a disappointment to the territorial forces but a great satisfaction to the Native Americans.

The main object of General Howard's mission, however, was to pacify, if possible, Cochise and the Chiricahua people. A former commissioner had made the effort but had been unable to get within 100 miles of the stronghold where Cochise had his camp. After a careful search, the General found a frontiersman named Tom Jeffords, reputed to be a friend of the Chiricahua, who agreed to help him. (On several occasions of attack, the Apache band had spared him.) Jeffords was willing to take General Howard to Cochise if he would go without any escort of soldiers. This was so agreed.

There were five in the party that, after days of hard riding, reached the Apache chief in his headquarters. The General and Jeffords were accompanied by Captain Sladen and two friendly Apache scouts, Chie and Ponce. These two men told Cochise who General Howard was, and what he had come for.

'Nobody wants peace more than I do,' said Cochise. '[The number of] my people keeps growing smaller and smaller. We will disappear from the face of the Earth if we do not have a good peace soon.'

Cochise was tired of constant foray and flight, and was ready to settle down, but he had sent his 12 sub-chiefs out into the field, and told Howard that the decision must await their return. The General was asked to stay with them 10 days or more.

LEFT: GERONIMO POSES DEFIANTLY FOR THE CAMERA WHILE IN THE CUSTODY OF THE US ARMY AT FORT SILL. *OPPOSITE:* THE CLASSIC PORTRAIT OF GERONIMO, STERNLY GRIPPING AN UNLOADED CARBINE. HE WAS PHOTOGRAPHED IN 1887 BY BEN WITTICK AT HIS ARIZONA STUDIOS.

83726

Howard was a lover of peace and respectful of the Native American people. As such, he had no fear of treachery. He settled down to make friends with them all, children as well as elders, sharing his meals with them and teaching a younger son of Cochise to sign his name 'Natchez.'

It was a name that was later to stand beside that of Geronimo as a symbol of Apache independence.

General Howard's peace efforts were successful. The various captains came in and a great council was held. The bands agreed to settle upon a Chiricahua reservation in southeastern Arizona with their friend Jeffords as their agent.

Cochise kept his promise of peace for the remainder of his life. He died in 1874 and passed on the obligation of leadership to his eldest son, who was likewise faithful.

However, by 1876 continued forays across the Mexican borders, not construed by the Chiricahua as a violation of their promise to Howard, led the US Government to abolish the reservation. An order was issued to the US Army to remove the band to the San Carlos reservation to the north. The Bureau of Indian Affairs was now endeavoring to carry out a 'policy of concentration.' This new policy sent a few Native Americans to the new reservation. It sent a greater number over the border into Mexico. Again the Indian Bureau had to ask the War Department to step in.

After the death of Cochise in 1874 and of his eldest son in 1876, the policy of concentration had negative results down on the Chiricahua reservation. Natchez, Cochise's younger son, and a charismatic 47-year-old chief named Geronimo (Goyathlay) led a group of Chiricahua south into Mexico.

They were soon joined by another Apache band led by Vittorio, who had left the Ojo Caliente reservation in the north. In both Mexico and the United States, the Apache under these leaders undertook guerrilla military actions. They knew every nook and corner in their rugged country and had little difficulty in living by a series of raids upon villages and wagon trains, eluding every attempt at capture.

Eventually, however, Geronimo and his band returned to Ojo Caliente and, being apprehended, settled down peaceably for a time on the San Carlos reservation. In 1882 he led a raid into Mexico, but was captured by General George Crook, and sent back again to San Carlos.

In 1884, Geronimo departed for more extensive raids, establishing a base of operations in the Sierra Madre below the Mexican border. His attentions to both nations in the matters of forays was quite impartial, so Mexico and the United States agreed to co-operate in capturing the Apache raiders — or rather to try to do so.

Vittorio was killed by Mexican troops, and Nana, his successor, was an old man. Geronimo, however, was in the prime of life, and Natchez was an unusually vigorous and stalwart young warrior.

In November 1885, a detachment sent out by General Crook met with Geronimo, Natchez, Nana, and other Chihuahua Apache chiefs in their Sierra Madre stronghold. The Apache proposed to surrender, as they had done on previous occasions, and Geronimo agreed to meet with Crook.

Geronimo told General Crook, when they met on 25 March 1886, that he would come in on the condition that the band go east for not more than two years. He felt he was in a position to dictate the terms of the agreement because they were fifteen miles below the border, well armed, well supplied with ammunition, and in a camp on a rocky hill that was a natural fortress. Only a few Apache came in sight at any time, but others were

ABOVE: THE MARCH 1886 PARLAY BETWEEN GERONIMO AND GENERAL CROOK'S DELEGATION. *RIGHT:* GERONIMO AND THE OTHER CHIRICAHUA PRISONERS BEFORE LEAVING ARIZONA FOR FORT SILL, LATER IN 1886.

on hand and watchful. They had come this far voluntarily and were as free as ever. They would come farther on their own terms or not at all.

General Crook agreed, told them to come in and telegraphed his decision to Washington. Three days later he received an answer saying that only unconditional surrender would be acceptable to President Grover Cleveland. Meanwhile, Geronimo and Natchez had tired of waiting and had ridden away with 35 of their followers.

Crook was also tired, and was dispirited when he received the telegram from headquarters. On 1 April 1886, he asked to be relieved from command. General Nelson 'Bearcoat' Miles, who had led the campaigns that defeated the Sioux and Nez Perce, was assigned to succeed him. Miles adopted the plan of spreading his men in small detachments throughout the territories of Arizona and New Mexico. His theory was that when Geronimo and his men came in on a raid they would be pursued by one group. Having safely eluded that one they would then find to their surprise that their trail was taken up by another.

General Miles credited most of his success during the summer of 1886 to the use of the heliostat, a device for signalling from station to station by means of sunlight flashed upon mirrors. Thousands of messages were sent from one to another of the 27 stations that he set up.

COPYRIGHT 1886. By C. S. Fly.

Meanwhile, Miles was decided that the Native Americans being held at Fort Apache, who were neither dismounted nor disarmed, should be sent into custody in the East. After a series of negotiations, dispatches, delegations, and discussions, the general was authorized to send them for a term of years to Fort Sill, Oklahoma as prisoners of war.

On 4 September 1886, Geronimo surrendered to Miles at Skeleton Canyon, Arizona. Natchez and his group soon came, and these Apache were removed to Fort Marion in Florida. In 1890, four years after these Native Americans were imprisoned, public sentiment was aroused to such a pitch that Congress ordered an investigation of the conditions of their imprisonment, and in 1894, with deaths among the women and children about double the normal rate, and because of unsanitary conditions, Geronimo and his band were moved to Fort Sill.

Geronimo, though technically still a prisoner of war, was allowed a certain amount of freedom after his relocation to Fort Sill. In 1905, at the age of 76, he was invited to ride in President Theodore Roosevelt's inaugural parade, and in 1908 he was invited to join Pawnee Bill's Wild West Show.

Geronimo died of pneumonia at Fort Sill on 17 February 1909. The Chiricahua continued to be held as military prisoners until 1914. By this time most of the 'prisoners' were too young to have memories of the wars, because, ironically, the children born at Fort Sill over the previous 28 years were also prisoners. In another bitter irony, one of the men enlisted in the United States Army served his time and was then returned to Fort Sill, where he died a military prisoner.

After 1914 the Chiricahua Apache were given permission to return to their old home on the reservation in the Southwest. Those who chose to remain in Oklahoma were settled on a reservation in that state.

Geronimo had the distinction of being the last Native American chief to lead his followers as a people independent of the authority of an outside government. His story rounds out an epic chapter of triumph and sorrow in the legacy of North America's Native people.

ABOVE: Marianetta, Geronimo's wife. *BELOW:* Geronimo with a group of Chiricahua warriors, circa 1880. *OPPOSITE:* A formal portrait of Geronimo at the age of 76, at about the same time that he was invited to ride in President Theodore Roosevelt's inaugural parade.

Index